THE

Real Moms

PLAYBOOK

LISA AUTRY

THE REAL MOMS PLAYBOOK

For more information, contact:

The Daughter Diaries | www.thedaughterdiary.com
Fig Factor Media, LLC | www.figfactormedia.com

Cover Design and Layout by Kevin Dakin
Printed in the United States of America

ISBN: 9780997160567
Library of Congress Number: 2021919527

Dedication

This Playbook is dedicated to all the women of the world, but especially the two women I'm raising to come into this world ready and able.

This, my girls, is for YOU.

May you be fierce. May you be kind.
May you be fulfilled. May you be balanced.

Table of Contents

Foreword 2

Introduction: The Plays to be a Balanced Boss Babe 5

1. YOUR MINDSET 12

Play #1: Saying Goodbye, Beautiful Intentions 13

Play #2: What Happened to HER? 16

Timeout: All My Single Ladies 21

2. YOUR NEST 24

Play #3: Throw Some Crap Away 25

3. YOUR TIME 41

Play #4: Get Your Shit Together, Woman 42

4. YOUR SELF-CARE 62

Play #5: Yeah, You Gotta Eat That, Stephanie 63

Play #6: Starve Your Demons, Fuel Your Fire 76

5. YOUR MONEY 88

Play #7: Why You're Broke AF 89

6. YOUR BOUNDARIES 106

Play #8: Pivot Real Good 107

Play #9: Zone Defense on Anxiety 115

Play #10: Ditch the Bitches 118

7. YOUR WIN 122

Becoming a Balanced Boss Babe 123

About the Author 127

Acknowledgements 128

Resources 131

My Intentional Transformation 133

Pursuing My Passion 143

Foreword

Almost ten years ago, I shared an office at an advertising agency in the Central Valley of California with an energizer bunny in her early twenties. Her name was Lisa Autry. She was all about finance and she was NEVER having kids.

Our work styles were vastly different. I used to joke that if you asked each of us to make a salad, I'd begin by asking what you wanted in it, starting with the base: spinach or mixed greens? Full of veggies or just a touch? Creamy dressing or vinaigrette? And before you could answer what your lettuce preferences were, Lisa would hand you a complete salad. What's in it? It doesn't matter. You asked for a salad, here you go.

We made the perfect pair, Lisa and A-lisa. Together, we could work efficiently and with artistry. I worked with the agency's creative team, and Lisa made sure everyone got their work done and got paid. I was also finishing graduate school at the time, studying to become an evidence-based coach for executives. When it came time to record my final exam for my coaching certification, I asked Lisa to be my coachee. I was learning how to slow people down for a living to help high achievers get clarity to move forward. Lisa was the perfect candidate. She was fun and easy to coach because she came with an openness for growth and constant desire to improve.

I had no idea how instrumental those early days laughing endlessly in a tiny office, building a lifelong friendship and coaching relationship, would be to this very moment in time. Fast forward to Lisa becoming a mom of two beautiful girls and a life-changer for women around the country. She's impacting women in their homes, in their relationships with their children, and their relationships with themselves.

When Lisa got the "baby bug" (very unexpectedly for both her and her husband

Matt, haha), she completely transformed her life to prepare for motherhood. She took a step back and looked at her health, her job, and every priority in her life to make sure they aligned with the woman, wife, and mom she wanted to become. When she had her first miscarriage, it was devastating. She had this magical grace and perseverance that carried her through to her next pregnancy. Lisa's overall health and pregnancy journeys have not been easy, to say the least. I'll let her share more (join her Facebook group to learn about all things Lisa), but today, she's balancing work and motherhood, and even her own struggle with endometriosis as a "balanced boss babe."

On the outside, Lisa looks like the woman who does it all. She actually does, though! I wish I could say, "I don't know how she does it," but she shares it in this book; she shares in her membership community (it's called "Tribe"—that's where you want to be if you're serious about transformation); and she shares as she learns, all over social media (perhaps that's how you found her). She's not a farce. She's the real deal.

You'll learn in this book that it wasn't always a seamless process. And even now, she'll be the first to tell you that she's tried to sell me her children multiple times! We've had virtual coaching sessions in her car late at night from her garage to get away from the madness. We've had cute little faces pop in and out of Zoom when it should be afternoon nap time. I've had pretend tea with her first daughter, Ava (who I personally believe was a genius by age two), and I had the pleasure of co-hosting the Sip 'n See for her second daughter, Mia (who gets her energy from Lisa).

Back in the day, I thought Lisa's house was always spotless, but it wasn't until recently I learned that every time I came over, it was a madhouse of shoving things in drawers and closets right before. (Can you relate?) Now, everything in her house has its place and each item is there to spark joy. Her life isn't perfect, but she's learned how to own her life and not let life own her. She's doing it, and you can too.

Lisa has a vision to take her message and her methods to a million women. This Playbook represents a lifetime of strengthening her innate ability to run an efficient life, the knowledge she's intentionally soaked up to become the best version of herself, and the humility that's helped her stay open to new possibilities along the way.

It's no accident that Lisa was one of my first paid coaching clients and later became one of my first vision production clients. You see, today as a vision producer, I help strong, high-achieving women get clarity on their huge visions, create a strategy, then get it all done, one step at a time. Lisa was made for greatness. She's getting it done, one step at a time.

Early on as my client, she saw herself as a mom who liked working out, liked organizing things, and liked money. Nothing particularly extraordinary, she thought. "Now what?" she asked me.

Her vision wasn't clear from the beginning. And she was busy trying to be all things for her family while not falling apart herself. Her vision first came from a desire to be present for every pivotal moment in her girls' lives, a desire to help others, make a living, and actually breathe from time to time to enjoy life. Her vision wasn't big... until it became something so colossal that it was oozing from the depths of her soul. Everything Lisa does comes from that place. She's filled with passion and ideas. She's figured out the basics to become an unstoppable force who wants to bring that passion out of both stay-at-home moms and working moms.

Are you ready to become unstoppable? You were made for greatness. You can take control over your health. You can get out of debt. You can have the relationships you desire. You can have a clutter-free home. You can get a good night's rest! You got this.

Lisa is a wise-beyond-her-years but still energized bunny, ready to take on the world with the systems to help you with your money, your time, your routines, and your energy, so that you can take on your world, too! The Real Mom's Playbook isn't just a bunch of inspirational fluff; it's a guide with practical tips that will remind you that you're not alone and that you truly can become unstoppable. Now, get ready to take notes and go be your badass self!

ALISA MANJARREZ
Vision Producer & Executive Coach, The Happy Cactus
thehappycactus.club

The Plays to be a Balanced Boss Babe

All good stories start at the beginning...

That is not where we are starting, however, because I need to throw you in the midst of fire for a second. (Don't worry, you won't get burned too badly.) And honestly, let's be real: motherhood is kind of a cluster that runs out of sequence anyway.

July 2018: I was getting ready for my Sip 'n See for my second-born daughter, Mia. (This is the fancy term for a baby shower after the baby has arrived in order to meet everyone.) I had worked all night long on a deadline that was due at 8 a.m. (Spoiler Alert: I didn't end up getting the project done until 7 p.m. the following night—yikes). One of the reasons I had worked all night was because my first-born daughter, Ava, would not go to sleep the night before. The other reason is Mia kept waking up every two hours crying, pulling me from my desk to care for her, which left me trying not to break down sobbing myself.

After the Sip 'n See, nearly losing it from pure exhaustion and sitting back down at my desk to work, I made a vow to myself. I vowed I would never do this again. I was going to learn how to manage my time better, be a better, more patient mother, and still make time for all the other duties within my life, because, let's be real, my house was a cluster at that point. I will learn so I can do better and be better. I deserve to be the BEST me possible.

But I couldn't quit working because I needed to help provide, since my husband was going to an extremely expensive university in order to earn his bachelor's degree. And I couldn't get rid of either of my kids to lessen the load, because which would I even get rid of? After all, they both piss me off on occasion. So, I needed to reevaluate: how the hell was I going to accomplish this? How could I be the person I needed to be without giving any of it up? (*Don't worry, that's the whole point of this book.*)

Present: I'm a mother of two beautiful and exhaustingly active girls, run three businesses out of my home, I'm the director of said home, (that's a fancy title I gave myself in lieu of "snack bitch"), and wife to a wonderful, doting husband that refuses to put his dishes into the dishwasher. (*It's okay, babe, we will continue to work on this.*)

THE MILLENNIAL MOM MYTH...

As moms, we are seemingly required to do it all and within the millennial generation, that rings truer now than ever before. We—more so than any generation in the past—now require two incomes to survive, so it seems. With rising economic costs, society dictating what the perfect life looks like, and attempting to "keep up with the Joneses," many households are swimming in debt, unfulfilled and just trying to make ends meet and looking towards a "better" tomorrow. And it's literally killing us...

The problem with this way of life is that tomorrow isn't going to come, unless we change our perceptions of what tomorrow looks like. It's up to you to decide that, and what we will be doing throughout the Playbook I've designed just for you. My struggles will become your triumphs.

The Millennial Mom Myth: I can have everything all the time and only then will my life be perfect, and I, be happy.

*The Millennial Mom Truth: When I get to the heart of what I desire in this life, I can have it all, be happy, fulfilled and not be a hot mess anymore, because I am no longer living someone else's life; I am living **my** best life.*

The title of this book is The Real Moms Playbook. You, my dear, are a real mom. You don't hide behind the facade of a perfectly polished Instagram or proclaim you live the perfectly charmed life. No, you are currently surviving. But together, we are going to get you to thriving, redefining your *real* motherhood. We can have our cake and eat it, too, I promise you.

My life can be rather chaotic and I, quite frankly, made it that way when I went and had kids. But I'm proud to say that *most days* I balance it all pretty dang well. My mornings start at 4:30 a.m., so I can have a little bit of "me time"—if you're wondering what that is, don't worry, we will cover that in a following segment—and then jump in to get ready to start everyone else's day. (Don't get scared away by a 4:30 wakeup time; I promise you this can work with a wake-up time to fit your needs.)

As mothers, our life really isn't our own, and it's kind of by our own design. It doesn't mean that it's wrong, it's just the damn truth, but it also doesn't mean you are living someone else's life. But this book isn't about commiserating or bitching and moaning (we do enough of that in our own heads); no, this book is about how to take action to become the mother you truly desire to become and need. The world depends upon it.

This book is the catalyst for your whole future, one you will create and cultivate. You have to do it and take accountability for it, own it, put the work in, and commit, because for the cost of this book, I am not going to show up at your doorstep and make you do it. (My house-call rates are way more costly.)

No one, not your spouse, your children, your friends, siblings, parents, whoever, can stop you from being the best version of YOU, and I'm going to address **all** the topics that limit us from that potential and how to fix the damn hamster wheel we find ourselves stuck spinning in. There is no one else identical to you in this world, so why waste it on halfhearted effort and the B.S. negativity we foster within us?

Remember that person you used to be before you had your children? Yeah, we are going to dig down deep and find that badass again. I know she's in there, but it's going to take a little bit of time, a tiny bit of effort, and a whole lot of faith.

HOW TO UTILIZE THE PLAYBOOK

The way this book is designed is by plays rather than chapters, with some fun little bonus bites thereafter. Why, you may ask? Because you will be taking these steps in order to become the best version of yourself, your unstoppable self that allows you to truly become the superwoman in your life. Don't skip around, because every bit of my success has been because I did these things in order, conquered them, and moved onward. This creates the beautiful, synergistic boss babe that is hiding within you. Only then can you become a balanced boss.

I've designed this to go at your own pace in succession but remember that momentum is your ally when it comes to completion of the intentional transformation.

Intentional Transformation: The action of a thorough shift in one's life, led with purpose and diligence to rise to one's best self.

This Playbook is meant to be used and taken everywhere with you. This is your guide and all your secrets to success, whether that success is monetary through a career or enjoying a hot cup of coffee in peace and quiet. I've also included ample space to make notes, journal, log your progress, and visually see your transformation as it occurs.

Within the Plays, there's a few main segments you will be conquering and themes throughout:

Your Mindset   Your Money

Your Nest   Your Boundaries

Your Time   Your Win

Your Self-Care

This ultimately leads you through your intentional transformation and development of the life you truly wish to live.

"But Lisa, how the hell can I add more to my already full plate?"

Great question. You will find out as you are going through this Playbook that you fill your time with a TON of useless crap that is not only hindering your potential but killing your vibe and energy. I call these space wasters, and you will be removing them because they don't make you happy or productive anyway. As you do this, you will find yourself becoming far more efficient, far more productive, and even have energy to spare for your spouse at night after your day is done (you know, to do whatever, maybe make another kid).

Also, I will be teaching you how to structure your day based on when it works best for YOU, and helping you build your own three pillars of success—home, routine, finances—so that you have time for self-care, finding your people and pursuing your passions in life.

"Who the hell is this chick, anyway?"

Also, an excellent question. Why should you take what I have to say as the gospel? First, you bought the book, so you're kind of in it now, aren't you?

Secondly, what do you have to lose? You obviously bought this because you are seeking something (or maybe it was gifted to you, which in that case maybe others are seeing your potential and room for growth). Worst case scenario, this beautiful book becomes a paperweight for one of your children's mediocre drawings.

Thirdly, in all my years within the professional world, the one thing I've found that everyone wants is more *time*. But since that's not able to be found anywhere, I have learned to make pretty damn good use of the time I have, and even applied my techniques to my clients, colleagues, and friends, and they've all seen amazing success as well through their own intentional transformations.

I've been you. I dove in the trenches when I had two babies while building three businesses. But within those trenches, I learned what it takes for me to be successful, feel fulfilled, and become the juggling boss that I knew was within me.

So, if you are at the end of your rope, take the leap, dive into this book, do the lessons, and be ready to make a lifelong change, and then please e-mail me your results, questions, or comments to info@thedaughterdiary.com. I'd love to see how this book impacted you.

Lastly, at the end of the Playbook, I've decided to include some of my must-haves to be a balanced boss. This includes programs I believe in and host, people to go to in order to get things handled, and some of the resources to move ahead in your life, as an extra, because I love and care. (Yes, I really do care, even if I will be mean-momming you.)

I truly believe women and mothers are better together, and so I'm asking you to believe in yourself enough to dive into this book with passion and persistence, because the life awaiting you on the other side of this intentional transformation is 120% worth every minute, digging yourself out of that literal trench you have yourself in.

Remember, you are already an inspiring mother, amazing wife, (or possibly recently single—in that case, congrats!), and talented individual, now it's time for you to realize it and live to your full and true potential.

————————

I want to preface this Playbook and forewarn you that there is some language held within. It's a Playbook, and we keep it real and raw and sometimes "poop show," just can't make the impact that "shitshow," does. If you are someone who shies away from some vulgarity, I recommend marking it out when you see it. It won't change the points I'm trying to make with the colorful language, and the impact it will make on your life will still be profound and transformative.

Before we dive in, I want to define a few terms that you are going to become quite comfortable with and hear more throughout the Playbook, so I want us all to be on the same page on what they mean throughout here:

Alignment: Knowing your purpose, what's important to you, and living it daily.

The Real Mom: The mom who is having to do it all for everyone—her kids, her spouse, her family and friends, even her boss—exhausted but still just keeps going. A Real Mom doesn't hide behind the facade of a perfectly polished Instagram or Facebook; she's real and raw and lets it show. She's the mom who feels so drained but will not back down, because deep down she knows she's worthy of this challenge in life.

Please note: This is not defined by any one classification of professionalism. Chaos within the real mom's life is prevalent in all career paths, whether you are a stay-at-home mom, working mom, or work-at-home mom.

Unstoppable: The ability to be relentless in the pursuit of passion and peace. An unstoppable mom follows the Playbook to a "T" and steps into her best self daily, dividing and conquering all the obstacles that get in her way.

Success: This means different things to different people. But within this Playbook, success is really the simplest of things like keeping the house tidy, squeezing in fitness, and enjoying your cup of coffee hot. (I like it cold anyway, but not everyone does.)

Balanced Boss Babe: This is what each mother is working towards and what all the beautiful steps within this Playbook ultimately lead to. A balanced boss babe knows what she wants, how to get it, and the meaning behind everything she does (even if at that moment she's a snack bitch).

Cross-Balance: The ability to move fluidly from one objective to another throughout the day without extreme overwhelm or crumbling chaos, creating a life of efficiency, effectiveness and success. A balanced boss babe learns how to cross-balance well and knows when to do it.

Mom Boss: A woman who is in control of her life. She knows what she wants and what it takes to make it happen.

––––––

Now, let's go kick some ass (*your own*).

Saying Goodbye, Beautiful Intentions

"Dear me, I'm done…"

I've always been all about journaling my feelings, and it started with my first diary when I was about seven years old. My mind has always been chaotic (I tell people all the time I'm ADHD, undiagnosed), and it was a way for me to understand what I was feeling, why I was feeling it, and setting a possible course of action for me to take in order to move forward.

And this is precisely why I have every one of my clients write a letter at the beginning of their own intentional transformation. I feel it's their defining moment to go all-in, a declaration to the universe of who they are and the fact that they are no longer backing down and being controlled by the chaos.

I had one client tell me it was her moment to say, "I'm done with my excuses that are holding me back." So, before you go onward in this journey of your new beginning, I want you to spend fifteen to twenty minutes having a heart-to-heart with yourself, finding closure and then releasing the old you to say hello to your new possibilities. Inner dialogue is huge for personal growth. There's room at the back of this Playbook for you to pour your heart out, so take a pause and do it before moving on. Because now we are women of action.

If you feel you don't have a way with words, I've shared with you my vague but hopefully inspiring letter to myself. Feel free to copy it down in the back (by hand) and make it your declaration, because, beautiful mama, we are going on the journey of a lifetime, and I need you to say you're no longer backing down, that you are truly unstoppable.

Dear me,

It's been a while since I've had this inner dialogue with you. I'm writing to you to say goodbye.

Goodbye to the limits that hold me back.

Goodbye to the excuses that I've been letting define me.

Goodbye to the belief that I am not worthy of living the life I deserve and desire.

My beautiful, irrational self, it's time to let go of the perceived notions that I cannot be all that I aspire to be, that it's a fallacy to push the boundaries on what I think I'm capable of.

I am limitless.

Excuses will not hold me.

I am worthy and more than enough.

I am unstoppable.

Today I am saying goodbye for my own closure and to say enough is enough. I'm going on this journey for myself, for every woman and for the future of us all.

I will invest in myself to express my capabilities.

I will guide through challenges with confidence and security.

I will find those to support me in my belief that I am worthy and allow me to live my life to the fullest.

Today I am going all-in; I will let faith guide me and be relentless in the pursuit of my highest self.

Here's to beautiful intentional transformations: let them pave the way to the me that's waiting.

Sincerely,

_____

Now, let's get to work.

Remember: This moment is one in which you will never live again, so pour your heart and feelings out. At the end, you will look back upon your transformation with this letter to see how unstoppable you've made yourself in your pursuit for alignment.

What Happened to HER?

---

*"Living a fulfilled life is about knowing what you
want out of it and then acting accordingly..."*

I went through the initial draft of this book and then realized I wanted to add something really important—like the most important. It's really the foundation of the mechanism for all that you will be learning within this whole transformation.

This whole book that you are going to be reading is diving into what you really want and how to get it. But first, we have to know WHAT it is we want, and I'll be showing you how to achieve it within this book.

When I began this journey, I really didn't know what I wanted. I never asked myself what it is I desired out of this life and what was really important to me.

I had lost a child.

I had struggled with postpartum depression.

I was diagnosed with endometriosis after a hernia repair.

I was weighed down by the presence of physical clutter.

I was stretching my days thin trying to fit it all in.

I was literally just surviving.

And I stopped one day and said, *"Something's gotta change, I'm at the end of my rope and can't do it anymore."* And since then, with nearly all of my clients, I've heard the same murmurings over and over again, pleadings to me, even. *What happened to her?*

As women and mothers, we don't ask ourselves often enough what it is we truly want in this life. These are the things behind all the superficial B.S. that we claim are important but don't spend enough time on. You know the superficial B.S. like the nice car, the boat, that extra bedroom that you've designated as the playroom even though the kids don't really play in there. All superficial B.S. that's intruding in on what's really important underneath it all.

So, before we dive into the intentional transformation itself, we are going to open up that inner dialogue once more and find out what's really important to you. Being unstoppable means knowing what you want and how to get it.

Your values are the things, both literal and figurative, that you hold dear, the principles and moral compass of all you desire, guiding you on your journey of life. And most of us aren't giving them another thought, much less living them.

Through The Real Moms Playbook, you will be putting these at the forefront DAILY. You will no longer be the passive, hot mess that society is dictating you to be, and you will live intentionally and purposefully. You will be designing your whole life around them in order to become unstoppable and balanced. Your lack of understanding and living your values is hindering you from becoming your best self, and now it's time to change it.

YOUR TOP FIVE

First, we need to sit down when it's nice and quiet and list out what's most important to you. Everything you can think of. You can get as specific as possible.

What's your list look like? Three items, eight items, thirty-five items? The bigger you can make it, the better it is to begin. We will narrow it down.

(Struggling? I've included a list at the end of this chapter to give you some ideas and to brainstorm.)

From there, see if you can group any together.

Do you notice patterns of what's important to you? Are you living them or not? (Be brutally honest with yourself, this is how we learn and grow). From there, whittle the

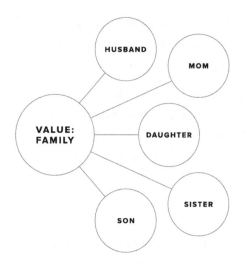

list down to your Top Five Values. These are the things that are most important to you, because if everything is of equal importance, then nothing is. Throughout this book, I will be pushing and guiding you on how to live your Top Five EVERY. SINGLE. DAY. This means structuring your home, routine, and finances to live in alignment with what you desire in this life.

At the end of this chapter, write down your final five in the space provided, your Top Five Values. (If you have a spouse, they will do it later. Right now is all about you and what you want for once!)

Please Note: Your values may change over time. Traveling was so important to me before kids, and now learning and growing at home is the most important to me currently. This will again change in another phase of life. That's literally life; we are always changing and evolving, so I recommend revisiting this exercise once a year or every couple of years. I like to at the end of the year when I'm reviewing the year's lessons and then planning ahead.

VALUE IDEAS

Sit down and list your top five values. I have listed some really good ones below, but there's a lot more. Feel free to include some that come to your mind that aren't listed here. The exercise is to determine what is MOST important to you, not what you think should be important.

To start the brainstorm, rate and rank the list below (one being the most important, ten the least), and then in the note section pull out and organize in order.

Please note: Some of these are physical things like travel, while others are more internal like peace and calm. How you interpret them into your daily life is dependent upon that inner dialogue and understanding how you wish to live (more to come, don't worry).

Accomplishment /
Achievement

Adventure/Travel

Balance

Challenge

Comfort

Community

Control

Convenience

Creativity

Discipline

Education

Elegance

Empathy

Excitement

Faith

Fame

Family

Focus

Freedom

Friendships

Fun

Giving

Gratitude

Growth

Happiness

Health

Honesty

Independence

Integrity

Love

Leadership

Loyalty

Peace

Philanthropy /
Donating

Pleasure

Presence

Privacy

Relationships

Religion / Spirituality

Rest

Safety / Security

Self-care

Success

Trust

Wealth

Wisdom

Work

NOTES / BRAIN DUMP:

_____

_____

_____

_____

_____

_____

_____

_____

MY TOP FIVE VALUES

1. _____

2. _____

3. _____

4. _____

5. _____

When we learn to live in alignment with our Top Five, this is when our true potential as a Real Mom is defined. We are able to do more with less time because our time is focused on the things that are most important, and that's extremely powerful. So, before you read further, stop and complete this lesson in full.

Now that you've worked on your head a little, let's dive into the home.

Timeout: All My Single Ladies

A TRIBUTE TO YOU

"On this journey of motherhood, you are never alone..."

Being seemingly alone on the journey of motherhood is hard, I know. While I am not single, having a husband who is oftentimes gone more than around puts a strain on us in our already chaotic lives. Whatever your circumstances are for becoming single with children, know that you are valued and heard. You are strong for leaving a potentially bad situation. You are seen for listening to your heart and letting it lead your life in a more positive direction. You are heard when you are struggling and surviving.

I decided to add this chapter as a timeout, because divorce and solo parenting is prevalent in our society today, which means we are under more pressure now than ever. And while I may be harsh in this book with what's to come, I want you to know that it's because I see your horizon for potential, I see your reality, and know your way forward, with or without a spouse. I salute you for being the mother and the father, while still being your best self as an individual.

So, Single Mama, know that you, too, need this intentional transformation, but here are a couple things I want you to keep in mind as you go through this process:

PRACTICE GRACE WITH YOURSELF

Motherhood is flipping hard, and even harder when you have an additional parenting role. So, while going through this transformation, practice grace with yourself. Push forward with unwavering faith and extraordinary effort with the intention of positively impacting your life, but understand that not every day will be sunshine and rainbows. That's just life.

Amidst the struggle, however, we rise to our best selves and prove to our mind, body, and soul that we conquer this life. So, if you are at a low point, practice grace but know it will be okay. Your current suffering is how you will overcome and conquer successfully within this transformation.

"Character cannot be developed in ease and quiet. Only through experience of trial and suffering can the soul be strengthened, ambition inspired and success achieved."

–Helen Keller

KNOW THAT CHAOS IS A NORM

Chaos will always strike, with or without a spouse. It's our ability to set that strong foundation, create a disciplined flow to our routine, get in control of our mindset, and become financially free that will help us to manage and mitigate the chaos daily. I recommend you utilize Hal Elrod's S.A.V.E.R.S. from *The Miracle Morning* at the start of each day. This will help you to pause and calm yourself in the midst of chaos striking.

This is how I embody his technique in order to capitalize in my daily life:

Start each morning with (even just a minute of each):

Silence - Take a few minutes to breathe and calm your mind during meditation

Affirmations - Write and reiterate your affirmations to fuel your fire for the coming day

Visualization - Plan your day to see and anticipate what the day will hold

Exercise - Move your body (I prefer just a few minutes stretch)

Reading - Pick up something (like this book!) that inspires and elevates

Scribing - Embrace that inner dialogue through journaling in the back of the book

No matter if you've gone through the intentional transformation or not, chaos is life, but this intentional transformation helps guide you on your route to balancing it effectively and efficiently and being the balanced boss babe of your days. **Our goal is to seek 85% control and 15% chaos management**. Accepting that chaos in life will help you to survive and advance through it.

SEEK SUPPORT WHEN ABLE

As women, we are conditioned to not ask for support and assistance, because we are superwomen that need to be able to do it all and do it all well. But the reality of life is that we cannot do it all to the best of our abilities. This book is the foundation for a calm, controlled environment, but you will still need to seek support sometimes, whether you need some self-care and silence, or need to go after that big promotion. (I will be discussing the power of delegating and you will use it!) Asking for help doesn't make you weak; it shows you realize the importance of community and balance.

JOIN THE TRIBE SO YOU ARE HEARD

I hope that you will come to realize through this book that I really give a shit about you and your life. And I want to continue to help take you to the next level. That is why I created the Mamas Unstoppable Tribe, so like-minded women can come together and work on leveling up their lives together on a consistent basis.

When you've done the steps in this book, you will see how much more calm, control, and clarity you have in this life, so that's a good time to seek support, take yourself to the next level with women who believe in you, and look forward to seeing yourself continue to grow. Find your Tribe, a place for you to be authentically you while elevating yourself with purpose and intention. In the words of Cara Alwill Leyba, *"When women come together, we all win,"*[1] because we are most definitely better together. Now, let's begin that transformation.

---

[1] Leyba, A. C. (2017). *Girl Code: Unlocking the Secrets to Success, Sanity, and Happiness for the Female Entrepreneur.* Portfolio.

PART 2

Your Nest

Throw Some Crap Away

NOT YOUR KIDS THOUGH

"Stuff is stressful and it's weighing you down..."

I've never been a person to lightly touch on a subject to spare those that are more sensitive than me (in case you didn't pick up on that within the intro). The reason for this is because I've never found it productive to beat around the bush when it comes to getting things accomplished. I'll be direct, I'll be honest, I'll be a little harsh at times—but ultimately, it's for your own good.

Don't get upset if you feel triggered or targeted, however, because we have to face these realities in order to move forward in a positive, productive direction. If you keep lying to yourself about your reality, then you are never going to learn and actually change your current situation. So having prefaced that to brace you, I'm now going to say this: *You have too much crap in your home. Seriously, way more crap than you actually need. Like, a lot of useless CRAP.* Whew, that felt, like, really good to get out of the way. #sorrynotsorry

If you look over at your kitchen counter right now and you can't make out if you have tile, granite, or some fancy marble-looking quartz, then you may have a problem. Physical items around your home clutter your mind, cloud your judgment, and bog down your motivation, and as a newly proclaimed mom boss, you don't need that weighing you down. If you want to accomplish big things in your life, then start within the home. That's where much of your immediate frustration and overwhelm will lie. Your home is your sanctuary, your place of peace, your foundation. Let's not crap all over it, alright?

Don't worry, you aren't alone and I'm going to show you how; that's the point of this book. If your home is already in order, congrats! But go through the motions and this process to make sure you are truly living a joy-sparked life.

About four years ago, I was blessed with my second daughter, Mia. Life during this time was rather chaotic, disorganized, and involved many sleepless nights and bouts of crying (from the kids *and* me). While it appeared that I had my ducks in a row on the outside while running my businesses, on the inside it was a flipping circus *(lions, tigers, and bears—oh my!)*. At this time, I was given a book from a dear friend and colleague (and she's now my executive coach and vision producer—the author of the foreword), Alisa. The book was about how to remove physical items from your home in a positive way, and the magical effects that will occur from it. Sound familiar? Maybe Marie Kondo rings a bell?

This was prior to the whole KonMari worldwide kick, and everyone jumping on the decluttering and joy-sparking bandwagon. But anyway, I was gifted this book titled, *The Life-Changing Magic of Tidying Up* [2]. I was instantly offended.

At the time, I remember I had been complaining to Alisa about how chaotic my life was, but I didn't need a book about throwing stuff away, I needed help becoming the ringleader of my carny crew. Alisa assured me it was right up my alley.

She didn't know at the time—and I thought I was hiding it from her rather well— that hidden within my home was complete and utter chaos in the form of stuff and clutter, packed into cabinets, thrown into drawers, and stuffed into closets.

At the time, I didn't see this as an issue, but I felt this way not just in life, but in motherhood. Definitely not the source of my chaos, the stuff was just sitting there. Still slightly pissed, I picked it up and read it. (She did give it to me after all, so it was free and maybe the reason you picked up this book.) I read it again. And again. Then I listened to it. Before I knew it, I was ripping apart my home in a frenzy to remove everything in my life that no longer suited me and going through my

---

[2] Kondō, M. (2014). *The Life-Changing Magic of Tidying Up: The Japanese Art of Decluttering and Organizing* (1st ed.). Ten Speed Press.

own joy-sparking journey. And the effects were freakin' unbelievable. Every item of clothing I removed that I no longer wanted, never liked, or never intended on wearing, created space not only within my closet, but also in my head.

The more clear my home became, the more clarity I was afforded about every aspect of my life. The more clear my home became, the more uplifted my spirits grew. *Clear the counter = clearing of the mind.*

The process took me roughly four weeks to go through every item in my home, but Marie believes it can take about six months. (What can I say, I'm an overachiever. Just kidding. Actually, I knew if I didn't do it in a frenzy, it wouldn't get done fully at all.) Marie suggests clearing your home by category versus rooms, this will ensure you remove any duplicates. (Do you really need four black peacoats?—maybe you do.)

I suggest picking up the book because she's far more eloquent than I ever will be, but I'm going to give you my personal breakdown of how to get it done in the four weeks that I did it in.

Please Note: Read this whole Play in full to understand the process in full. It's exciting to jump in, but it's most important to understand not only how but why we are doing this process. So, let's dive in, shall we?

THE FOUR-STEP PROGRAM

Anyone that knows me knows I'm all about systems. Systems are sexy. Systems are disciplined. Systems are machines that run without much thought. And we want the home to operate like a machine in order to be efficient and clear and keep the carnival you call your family from running amok.

In order to clear your home of the clutter, we are going to complete the following decluttering system:

1. Gather - pull all your items together

2. Discard - determine what stays and what goes

3. Organize - organize what remains

4. Maintain - become a woman of proactive action

The first three steps are the act of removing the clutter; the final step is ensuring you never have to read this chapter again and redo the process, because we have way bigger fish to fry on this journey of motherhood than constantly picking up messes.

Let's review the individual steps:

STEP 1 - GATHER IT, GIRL

First, you must gather ALL items by category. I'll talk about categorical order at the end of this segment, and there's plenty of room to track your progress to get it done. For now, I'm just getting you to understand how the process works.

GATHER, GATHER, GATHER

This means searching every place that that specific category may be. When diving into clothes, don't only go through your closet and dresser, but also the coat closet, car, mom's house, the toy box, wherever more of this category may be. This is the **most** important step, as it helps you gain an understanding of the volume of what you have, as well as who you are as an individual (maybe you're just discovering this joy-filled woman).

For every client that has completed this task (including myself), it was a moment of realization, one that provided clarity and closure on our habits, the beliefs we hold about ourselves, and defined who we wish to become in the future. It's truly impactful.

Once you bring all the items together, lay them in nice piles according to sub-categories. This ensures you go through them most effectively and efficiently and allows you to visually feel and see the volume of what you own. This brings us to discarding (my favorite part).

STEP 2 - DISCARD WHAT WEIGHS YOU DOWN

Be decisive about this and don't overthink it. Grab it, get a feel for it, and decide immediately if it stays or goes.

Marie talks about the beautiful energy and electricity you will feel when you proceed through the magical process. And, I promise you, you actually do feel things for the items you maintain within your home.

What about the kids?

"Lisa, this process won't work. The tiny children I've created live here and are professional mess makers..."

Hence, why the title warns you NOT to throw them away. I get asked all the time what to do about kid's things because oftentimes they won't part with it.

My tip: Don't force them. It's not up to you to sneak it away under the cover of darkness to later pretend it's just hidden somewhere in the house. It actually creates mistrust, so my recommendation is to involve them in their tidy process, let them see their volume, give them options, but let them know nothing new can come in until some old goes.

It'll get them to discern what's truly important, developing emotional intelligence. Oftentimes my own kids just want to see where their things go, so donating them makes them feel important and giving. My oldest is sentimental, and so, naturally, for her, parting with things becomes more of a challenge and that's why we discuss it.

Get to know your kids and what process they require and the comfort level they have for discarding things.

If you feel nothing or negatively about something, then it's probably time for it to go. I've had clients who had guilt for all the unused items they maintained, while others saw it as an opportunity to move onward, quickly knowing they didn't care for the item. Everyone, I've noticed, has different feelings about the things that occupy their space. I know for me, what I released created opportunity for new moments and memories with new things, and to me, that was pretty exciting.

If it stays, set it aside to complete during the organization step—but don't start organizing... yet! If it goes, determine if it gets sold, donated, or tossed. Depending on the condition of the items, you might even make some money during this process.

I donated ten carloads, over eighty bags AND went on to sell another $4,000 worth of items, and I wasn't even considered a hoarder by any means. *Can you say win?!*

Discarding means:

Toss   Sell   Donate

The biggest impact of all was that I started to get a real and true understanding of who I was as an individual. And at this point, now knowing your values, your stuff will begin to become a direct reflection of that.

GO WITH YOUR GUT

When deciding if something stayed or left, I determined I would base clothes on the likeliness of me wearing them again—was I really going to lose the baby weight? Spoiler alert, you will and there's a chapter on this—or if I felt good in it whenever I wore it. If I didn't wear something in a year, it immediately was discarded because it meant I was holding on to something that was meant to move onward. But I always went with my gut on how I felt about items, and I want you to hone in on this too.

Don't feel guilty if something has gone unused and you want to discard it. Marie talks about how it fulfilled its purpose by the feelings you received when you bought it or the excitement and appreciation when it's an item you received, even if it never really got worn or used. I found this great closure for me, so I didn't feel wasteful or unappreciative. And it's going to continue its journey elsewhere, after all.

When assessing something for joy that really has no emotional attachment, ask yourself: Do I like this product, is it necessary, or will I ever eat this food? I found a lot had been hiding in my pantry that I was never planning on eating. Note to self: Don't buy in bulk unless you know you like it.

The trick for me (and for all of the clients I've seen guided through this process) was to get the discarded items out of my house as quickly as possible. Get it out of your sight and out of your mind. You will instantly be granted more clarity, and this will help you in the organizing phase if you aren't shuffling around bags for

Goodwill/Disabled Army Veterans Charity or garage sale items. *Grab it, decide, act, and move onward.*

"DO I HAVE TO GET RID OF EVERYTHING?!"

I get this question every single time I on-ramp a client to start the process. This is not the journey towards minimalism (unless that's your intent), but rather the understanding of what makes you happy and is useful within your life. So no, this process is not about throwing everything away or having your most prized possessions ripped out of your claws, but about lovingly, joyfully freeing yourself from the weight of your physical items. If it brings you joy, then keep it!

Once you remove everything that no longer brings you joy, has served its purpose, or you have no desire to keep, then we move on to organizing.

STEP 3 · OPTIMAL ORGANIZATION

Now, once you've removed everything that's going bye-bye, you may have substantially less than what you started with. This is a good indication that you need to do more soul searching within your value system to determine what joy means for you. My organizational process is really simple and is based on ease of accessing the item and position within the home. If it's hard to get to when you need to use it, you won't put it away. Tip: You don't need more storage; you need less to store. Once I was done with the discarding process, I ended up donating a dozen storage bins that I always "felt I needed" or were "a cute way to hide all my crap." Keep it simple, make it cute if you want to, but not because you are trying to strategically hide all the stuff that is clouding your mind and judgment. That is not how you think about your stuff anymore, remember.

ORGANIZATIONAL TIPS BASED ON CATEGORIES

CLOTHING & ACCESSORIES:

For hanging items, I like to sub-categorize by types of clothing: long dresses, bulky coats, blouses, etc. Like Marie talks about, it creates a sweeping motion within your closet space and makes it more visually appealing. Let your space and how you think define how it functions. Remember: Think Easy!

Evenly space all hung items to give a nice aesthetic and make it easier to access without disrupting all the other items within. It'll also remind you where it sits when it's time to return it from the laundry.

I highly recommend YouTube for videos on how to fold via the KonMari Method™ because it will aid you greatly in the ability to pack a lot in small spaces (if you didn't declutter a whole lot). It's a smart use of limited storage, and the clothes maintain perfect shape within their tiny, folded boxes.

For accessories, make it fun but not overwhelming. Do you like to see your jewelry and shoes out, or more so concealed? My jewelry is in my bedside drawer in cute dividers so I can quickly grab and go, and my shoes are lined in my closet, visible and accessible. Maybe for you, you like your jewelry hung up or on display. I do prefer my clients take their shoes out of the shoeboxes; be proud of your items and don't hide them away! See, make it easy.

BOOKS:

Let the stories accent your life and remind you of the tales they hold within. I love physical books, everything from the touch, feel, and smell, and always make notes within (which is one of the reasons I leave so many spaces for you ladies in this Playbook). If you ever catch one of my Facebook Lives, you'll see them strategically decorating my shelves so when I walk past, I can reflect on all they contain within and all I've learned from them. Books are beautiful; let them shine. Can't stand too many physical books? Switch to digital tucked out of sight.

PAPERS:

Paper is persistent and always keeps flowing into your home, so you must have a sustainable system that works for you and allows you to be a maintenance maven. This is the organizational system I practice and teach to all of my clients:

1. Deep File (Fireproof or Storage Bin)

    - The last seven years of filed taxes with backup documentation

    - Birth certificates / Marriage documentation

    - Life insurance

    - Important and sensitive medical records

    - Loan documentation

2. Highly Accessed

- Open health insurance claims

- Current tax year receipts

- Outstanding bills

- Current year paid bills for the year

- Manuals you MUST have (do you really need the one for the sound machine? No.)

KOMONO:

What is Komono? It means miscellaneous items and is everything not held within all the remaining categories and also typically the biggest burden of clutter. From bedding and toiletries to office and kitchen, this category is the largest and most overwhelming for most families. The subcategories within this category are all dependent on the areas within your home, but here's some basic rules and guidelines for you to follow:

KEEP LIKE WITH LIKE

When you scatter categorical items throughout the whole house, it's harder to find and harder to maintain. Take your brain out of the daily management and find a home for the specific item, ideally with its relatives, like keeping all tape, all tools, all plates, all bedding with its friends (they don't want to be lonely!); it'll make your life easier to maintain.

FLOOR IS FOR FEET, NOT STORAGE

Keep items off the floor that don't belong on the floor. This is more visually appealing and makes it far easier to clean. You don't live in a storage facility—it's your home.

MAKE IT EASY TO ACCESS

Being busy mothers, we must lead the path of least resistance because we don't need the home to be just another burden in our lives. We need it to function and flow, and that means making highly accessed items easy to access (aka easy to put back).

SENTIMENTAL:

These are the things near and dear to your heart, so let them shine! I like to hide my little mementos throughout the house, so I'm always smiling. I have a stone carving of a wolf (my favorite animal) from my childhood in my reading corner and a quote that brings me joy in my bedside drawer. If they are stuffed away in a box, you won't enjoy them. Whatever you are proud of, bring it out!

DIGITAL:

Determine an easy filing system for emails, digital photos, and documents. I like Google Drive for my documents and Google Photos to organize and archive my photos by events and people. Keep items off your desktop—that's another physical space that's overwhelming to manage!

STEP 4 - MAINTENANCE MAVEN MODE

Now, I'm going to help you learn how to keep up with your home and daily life. I'm going to make you the most badass maintenance maven this world has even seen.

> **Maintenance Maven:** A badass mom who is the expert in keeping her home tidy without extreme effort. This woman works smarter rather than harder in her spaces.

NO more dirty dishes in the sink.

NO more laundry constantly overflowing from the hamper.

NO more toys scattered throughout the house.

Remember, systems are sexy, and you will create a system for your home that operates for you and doesn't rule you. Overthinking the simplest things will only cloud your mind and keep you from growing into your most unstoppable self, so we are going to officially stop that. Discipline will equate to your true freedom when you create rules to live by.

ROUTINE SCHEDULE

When you have a system, a home just runs.

Create a routine for these items:

- Process Mail Daily (Decide if you act now, file for later or immediately discard)

- Make Bed Every Morning (Declare to the world your day has begun)

- For the Kitchen Follow Prep, Cook, Eat, Clean style (Always manageable)

- Cleaning your home (Full/light clean weekly)

- Laundry day(s) (I recommend twice a week)

LAUNDRY ROUTINE

I recommend two times (no more than three) a week to wash clothes and towels. This is all dependent upon how many clothes you have but try to ensure you have enough to remove the burden of consistently doing laundry. Immediately transition laundry once washed and dried, and then STAND while folding at a counter so you can immediately transitionally flow into putting it away. It makes you fold faster and creates less resistance walking and putting them back in their home. Every other week is bedding. Don't watch TV while folding because you will be folding until your first-born heads off to college (and she's currently five).

Rules:

Stand up and elevated   Remove distractions   Immediately put away

CLEANING ROUTINE

Pick a day in which you clean. If you clean something every single day, guess what? Your home will never feel finished—true story. Pick a day, turn on a podcast and get to work. If your kids are old enough, put them to work too. Let them become experts in a piece of the chores. Everyone takes a part in maintaining the home in which they reside.

Tip: Clean by category, **not** room. Just how you went through the discarding process, you will do the same in maintenance maven mode. That means dusting the whole house, then moving to cleaning all the sinks, you'll then wipe all the counters, clean all the toilets, vacuum all the floors, and mop all the areas. This creates proficiency in the task at hand and alleviates the resistance (working smarter, not harder).

———————

But I don't clean my own home...

If you are someone who doesn't clean your own home, I highly recommend starting. Why? I used to have a housekeeper, and I realized I loved and appreciated my home that much more once I put the work in myself. And now I use it as personal development time by listening to podcasts, so it's a double win. It also gives me the chance to delegate to my girls, so they can feel accountable for their spaces and allows them to earn allowance. It's their home too, let them be a part of maintaining it. Give them a job and have them own it.

POST-PLAY PICK-UP / TRANSITIONAL TIDY

You know how to keep up on your home and ultimately your life? You clean as you go. This means dishes, toys, papers, mail, anything that can pile up over the course of the day. Cook a meal? Clean right after that meal before transitioning onward. Kids get out toys? Make them clean up in full before moving on to the next activity. Grab the mail? Process it immediately and file it.

While this isn't a completely new concept, it is something that's highly impactful. This will give you the sense of clarity, productivity, and efficiency, so that you can produce in other areas of your life. It's also harder to go back to something when you feel like you are already done with it, without actually being done with it. Put the items back in their home. They want to rest too! Lost your keys before? How long did it take to find them? Yeah, you could have finished another objective in the time it took you to find those damn keys.

THE TEN-MINUTE TIDY

Once you become the maintenance maven I know you truly are, then the only other thing is the quick ten-minute tidy before bed. These are for things that happened to randomly get set down or toys that got missed in transition (like under the couch where everything seems to disappear). If you forgot to take out the trash post-meal, you can do this now.

Why do we do this? Because tidying before bed signals to you that it's time to rest, relax, and decompress since you have successfully closed out your day. Also, nothing is more annoying than waking the next day to messes everywhere and kicking around toys in the dark, heading to the coffee pot in that half-asleep stupor.

BECOMING PICKY ABOUT THE CLUTTER

Of course, you will continue to welcome new items in your home like food, clothing, maybe new furniture pieces, or maybe even another child, which means accumulation of more stuff. But after the process is complete, it's important to understand your spending habits and be selective in regard to the new items you bring into your home.

Remember: Things now only come into your home that spark joy.

Answer these questions (in your head or on paper) prior to bringing new items in your home:

1. Why do I feel the need to buy this?

2. Does this item bring me joy or is it useful to me?

3. Does the act of spending money bring me happiness or is that actual item needed?

4. Would I be able to replace the act of buying this thing with an activity that brings me joy that does not clutter my home?

Time to Take Action

You can do one of two things with this process since it's lengthy:

1. Complete this process now (there's a checklist below)

2. Choose to finish the book and immediately come back to this segment and complete in full (recommended)

PRE-WORK - DETERMINING YOUR DESIRES

Before you dive into this process, it's time to have that inner dialogue with yourself once more (we keep doing it, I know!).

Answer these questions to get a better understanding of yourself:

1. What do my values mean to me within my home?

_____

_____

_____

2. How does my home currently make me feel?

_____

_____

_____

3. What areas within my home do I struggle with and why?

_____

_____

_____

4. How do I hope my home will feel and function at the end of this process?

_____

_____

_____

THE CATEGORICAL QUEEN - THE ART OF DISCARDING BY CATEGORY

As Marie discusses, you want to move in categorical order, starting with least sentimental during the discarding process. We go by category to effectively review all of that item and ensure there are no duplicates. Why? It's easier to start the process and follow through if you practice that discarding muscle (it's science).

Here's the simple outline for categories to check off as you go along with a timeline to follow my four-week path. This is her process, but I just guide you on how I maximized my time while doing it. Most of my clients take anywhere between four to eight months. For me, however, being a business owner, I knew if I didn't get it done fast, I would never finish. So, this timeline below is catering to those individuals. Go at the pace that you feel most comfortable with.

You may have more or less depending on your life:

WEEK 1 (4 DAYS)

- [ ] Clothes & Accessories (your own)
  - [ ] Tops (long and short)
  - [ ] Bottoms (long and short)
  - [ ] Dresses
  - [ ] Undergarments (underwear and bras)
  - [ ] Socks
  - [ ] Coats
  - [ ] Lingerie
  - [ ] Bathing suits
  - [ ] Athletic apparel

WEEK 1 – 2 (3 DAYS)

- [ ] Books (all types of books, even cookbooks)

WEEK 2 (5 DAYS)

- [ ] Papers (personal & business, if applicable)

WEEK 2 – 3 (10 DAYS)

- [ ] Miscellaneous
  - [ ] Toiletries
  - [ ] Towels
  - [ ] Bedding

- [ ] Cleaning Supplies
- [ ] Office Supplies
- [ ] Crafts & Art Supplies
- [ ] Outdoor Equipment
- [ ] Toys
- [ ] Kitchen

WEEK 3 – 4 (8 DAYS)

- [ ] Sentimental
  - [ ] Photos
  - [ ] Yearbooks
  - [ ] Diaries / Letters
  - [ ] Awards
  - [ ] Drawings
  - [ ] Mementos

BONUS WEEK:

- [ ] Digital
  - [ ] Documents
  - [ ] Digital Photos
  - [ ] Emails

Marie goes far more in-depth on this, but I think this can give you the gist to get going.

It will look worse before it gets better—that means you are doing it correctly!

PART 3

Your Time

Get Your Shit Together, Woman

THE ART OF MANAGING YOUR TIME

"Everyone has the same 1,440 minutes per day. How are you using yours?"

I'm going to paint you a little word picture and you see if it resonates with you…

You wake up after your alarm with two snoozes. You roll out of bed and quickly realize both you and the kids will be late, so you take a haphazard shower while brushing your teeth. You dash out of the shower and stare blankly at all the clothes you hate (because, well, nothing fits since you still have about fifteen pounds of postpartum baby weight from eight years ago). You grab the same plain black shirt because you know what to expect with it, and it doesn't have coffee stains or spit-up on it.

You apply "It's a 10" dry shampoo for the fourth day in a row because, well, that's really all you've got time for today, and enough makeup so as few people as possible ask if you're sleep-deprived, and to hide the crow's feet screaming at you in the mirror.

You run to the kitchen to start packing breakfast, because who has time to eat here, get the kids up and demand they get dressed, and brush their teeth halfway decent so they don't kill their classmates. You hear your youngest screaming at the railing of their crib, but you have to start your coffee and get your "energy and clarity" for the day. You spill coffee grounds all over, but that's okay because you'll feel better and like yourself again once you take that first sip. You grab your baby, rush back to the kitchen to finish packing lunch and breakfast, start receiving emails, texts, and calls from work, screaming at your kids and then spill your coffee all over yourself... **Good morning—not.**

And you do this around five times a week, do a shitty job of cleaning on Saturday, do thirty million loads of laundry on Sunday, and then start this sick cycle all over again. This is not your life… or not how it should be anyway.

Pushed to the Limits

With the onset of the COVID Quarantine in 2020, the work/home balance has been pushed even further to the limits. You may be fully working from home now when you used to leave and I will tell you, while it's definitely harder, if you follow the steps within this book, it will most definitely feel easier. This is how I've run three businesses out of my home with two little ones. Easy? No. Achievable? Yes.

Your routine (or lack thereof) is what is holding you back on a daily basis from moving forward into unstoppable mom mode. Maybe you don't leave the home at all and work, but your life seems chaotic, nonetheless. When you live amidst chaos, after a while, you kind of just assume that's how life is supposed to be. But remember, mediocrity doesn't suit you; it's holding you back from your truest potential and your best self, the unstoppable real mom I keep mentioning who is a balanced boss of her days.

This Playbook is teaching you how to lead the unconventional life, one that grants you the ability to see the glass as half-full and accomplish all that's of importance to you. I was told one time by a mean mom that you can't have a schedule and routine for children because that's not how they operate. Now I see why she had several children who acted out in anger and constantly got into trouble. Children don't like to wonder what's coming next. Discipline and order calm the soul and the same goes for you. *Your discipline ultimately will become your freedom from the shackles of your current chaos.* Life is full of so many unknowns, but your daily routine structure should not be one of them.

Consistency is QUEEN in YOUR Castle

When I dove into my own consistent routine, I found there was a parallel on how I ended my day and the success I would see the following day. The habitual cycle of chaos we place ourselves in is what is holding us back. Life will always be chaotic when there's people in it, so how we manage and mitigate it is KEY.

And since you've already kicked the clutter, you are prepared to move forward with building a life within that newly cleaned castle (once you go through the previous play—you can't build a beautiful life on a faulty foundation).

BECOMING A ROUTINE QUEEN

The great news is we don't have to let chaos rule us from sunrise to sunset (and if your kids are like mine, in the nighttime, too). Does that mean chaos won't strike? No, life will always happen, but within Play #8: Pivot Real Good, I'll be discussing how to realign when shit hits the fan.

I wasn't always a routine queen. I used to be someone that very much lived in chaos from sunrise to sunset and thought that was just the way life was with kids. I mean, society tells us that it's supposed to be that way, anyway. The minute I adjusted my perspective and established order that cultivated function and flow, my girls changed their whole attitudes and how they saw life, including their sleep habits. They went from sleep-deprived, emotional little animals, to consistent sleepers (still emotional little animals). They were happier, more inquisitive, and more consistent in their moods, too, and that is always a plus! True story.

Now is your time to adjust perspective and establish order. You are going to become the queen of your castle starting **today**. It's not easy to get consistency down, but once you develop that foundation, order will follow, and you'll instantly feel calmer and more controlled. And guess what? Suddenly, you will feel as though more time has magically appeared in your life, even though we all get the same 1,440 minutes in a day. I'm not kidding.

Imagine just having a whole afternoon playing on the floor with your kids without laundry piled up. Imagine just being able to lay across the couch and read a book without dishes overflowing in the sink. Imagine going for a walk as a family without thinking about mounds of work on your desk. The purpose of this whole Play is to create structure, order, and establish consistency in order to gain control over your life (with a little practice to make them habits).

Please Note: This whole segment is packed full of research and can seem rather overwhelming at times. When it's time to take action, you'll be told to take action, and it will continue to propel you forward. This is a segment you want to conquer, and it is worth the time and energy that it takes to become aligned (and balanced) in your daily life.

Go with the Flow

I recently had a client tell me in her on-ramp call that she was spontaneous in nature, so a routine wouldn't work for her.

I get it: structures and routines feel rigid. But when done right, they can be fluid and successful without making you feel STUCK. If you are spontaneous in nature, read between the lines on this Play, because discipline with your time and energy will grant you the freedom to leverage your time as you see fit.

ONE: SLEEP

Your lack of sleep is literally killing you. It's killing your patience. It's killing your productivity. It's killing the elasticity in your skin, causing those crow's feet. It's killing the pigment in your hair, causing greys. Straight. Up. Killing. You.

Most of us think it's strictly our kids doing this, but it's mostly because we are self-sabotaging our own natural flow of energy and failing to practice our best sleep habits, and this really started when we were teenagers thinking we knew better when our parents told us "lights out."

Whenever I begin working with clients on their routine and establishing disciplined flow within their lives, I always start with clarity around sleep. Why? Because it's the biggest productivity killer of all time.

OBJECTIVE 1: DON'T HIT THE SNOOZE

According to Michael Breus, clinical psychologist and sleep expert, hitting snooze is your worst enemy. Each time we are woken from a deeper sleep state, it triggers a response in your system to awaken and fight. (We are really all like cave people still.) This elevates both your adrenaline and cortisol levels, which jumpstart your body into action. When you do this over and over in a five to fifteen minute period, you are releasing adrenaline and cortisol over and over, shocking your system repeatedly, killing your restorative state (often why you feel like a zombie after that extra ten minutes for the whole rest of the day).[3]

Put your alarm far enough away to hear it, but where it requires you to fully get up to turn it off, making you more apt to stay up and keeping you from repeating the wake and scare cycle. Want to take it a step further? Don't use an alarm at all but a Wake-Up or Sunrise System that simulates the sun rising in your dark room. This helps you kick the sleep inertia (the grogginess you feel upon waking) in a more natural and calm way faster.

OBJECTIVE 2: BE ACTIVE DURING THE DAY

An active lifestyle and quality of sleep go hand-in-hand. According to Charlene Gamaldo, MD, medical director of Johns Hopkins Center for Sleep at Howard County General Hospital, "Moderate aerobic exercise increases the amount of slow wave sleep you get. Slow wave sleep refers to deep sleep, where the brain and body have a chance to rejuvenate."[4] Just being intentional about moving more and getting

---

[3] Breus, Michael. PhD. 2019. *Reasons to Skip the Snooze Button.* Psychology Today. https://www.psychologytoday.com/us/blog/sleep-newzzz/201907/reasons-skip-the-snooze-button

[4] John Hopkins Medicine. 2021. *Exercising for Better Sleep.* Psychology Today. https://www.hopkinsmedicine.org/health/wellness-and-prevention/exercising-for-better-sleep

steps in will help with this direction. Dance with your kids, track your steps, embrace the moment, and move! We will be discussing this in the next segment, Play #5.

OBJECTIVE 3: REMOVE THE CHAOS

Within an hour of your sleep time, turn off social media and the television, removing the chaos and clutter from your mind. The bright lights actually stimulate your brain, making it harder to get into sleep mode. And let's be real: that argument you always seem to get into on Facebook elevates your heart rate and keeps you from calming down.

This is your self-care period, known as your Power Down Hour, before going into your restorative state. So pick up a book, take a bath, reflect by journaling, and plan for tomorrow. Set yourself up for peace and sleep success.

REFLECT & PLAN

During Power Down Hour, I always have my clients in Mamas Unstoppable Tribe (my membership community)—I do this, too—reflect on the day, their accomplishments and success, and express gratitude for the things they appreciate in their life. Then we get to anticipating what is to come. In planning for tomorrow, closing out the day in anticipation for the next will have you waking with excitement and intentional purpose.

Your Power Down Checklist Rules:

☐ Reflect

☐ Express Gratitude

☐ Plan

OBJECTIVE 4: GET CONSISTENT WITH IT

Easier said than done, right? Don't worry… that's exactly what we will be talking about. So how do we get good, consistent sleep when we don't have a good, consistent routine? I know, it feels weird, but as we build, it will all fall in line.

First, you need to understand your natural ebb and flow of energy. Ever notice how certain periods during the day you feel groggy and foggy, and other periods more alert and focused? Yeah, that's your genetic makeup, your Chronotype, at work.

Michael Breus, the author of *The Power of When*, dives into our genetic makeup and how to function best based on WHEN we function best. It's not just about what you do, but when you do it that's the key.

As Michael states, we are one of four Chronotypes:

Dolphin - The Insomniac

Bear - The Social Creature

Lion - The Early Riser

Wolf - The Night Creature

Every Chronotype requires a different amount of sleep to properly function. Bears need the most at eight hours, while dolphins can function well within six hours. When my results came back Lion, I then understood why I always wake up hungry and why my energy ran out midday, which then helped me to learn that if I scheduled my fitness time at 5:00 p.m., I could have enough energy to get through the evening.

When I'm helping my clients become the queens of their routine, I help them understand how to live balanced lives, and that means getting enough sleep at their ideal time, as well as doing specific tasks at the right time in flow with their energy.

Being moms, we cannot always adhere to our Chronotype's ideal sleep and wake times. So instead of telling you when you should go to sleep and when you should wake, here's the ideal number of hours your Chronotype should be aiming for, so you have the energy needed to be the boss of your days:

DOLPHIN - THE INSOMNIAC

SLEEP GOAL: 6 HOURS

As someone who has a difficult time going to sleep and staying asleep (you wake often), shooting for a solid six hours will give you enough sleep you need in order to properly function at a decent level. You will always be tired when you wake though, that's just the dolphin way, so make sure you wake and get moving to help combat that (and don't use coffee as a Band-Aid, it makes it worse). Fitness is your friend!

LION - THE EARLY RISER

SLEEP GOAL: 7 – 7.5 HOURS

Being early risers, Lions love to get to bed early. But make sure not to go too early, so you can still keep up with social Bears. Being active in the early afternoon helps keep me awake until a decent hour, and still gives me the level of sleep I require. The same goes for all my Lion clients, as well. Deep thinking in the morning, workout in the evening.

BEAR - THE SOCIAL CREATURE

SLEEP GOAL: 8 HOURS

Bears, my social friends. Our society is built all around you and your way of life, and true to your animal nature, you need plenty of sleep. Try to get to bed at a decent hour so you can wake and be a mom boss the next day having achieved that full eight hours you need! Stay out late one night? Don't sleep in but maintain your consistent wake time—your body will adjust. Roll out of bed and get moving!

WOLF - THE NIGHT ENERGIZER

SLEEP GOAL: 7 – 7.5 HOURS[5]

All my Wolf friends live for the nightlife—that's who you are. As moms, however, this makes it a challenge, so push it back so that you can still rise with your little ones and be able to function. While you don't need as much sleep as Bears, you still need a decent amount, so adjust accordingly while still catering to your nighttime nature. A good Power Down Hour is crucial for your success on getting to sleep (more on that later).

Don't know who you are? Make sure you go to Michael's site, thepowerofwhenquiz.com, and take the chronotype test.

---

[5] PhD, B. M., & Md, M. O. C. (2019). *The Power of When: Discover Your Chronotype—and Learn the Best Time to Eat Lunch, Ask for a Raise, Have Sex, Write a Novel, Take Your Meds, and More* (Illustrated ed.). Little, Brown Spark.

My chronotype is: _____

Some things about my Chronotype:

_____

_____

_____

I also highly recommend getting his book and becoming an expert in your Chronotype, and how to make all the necessary adjustments in just four weeks to live fully aligned, as my analysis is only to get you going on the right step forward and not comprehensive of everything about your genetic bio-time.

Your body needs to restore, so look at your ideal times and see how far you are off and how much (or how little) sleep you are getting. Start tracking it over the next week to see what adjustments need to be made.

THE RESET

Many of us are not living within our circadian rhythm (the internal process that regulates our sleep). That leads to chronic fatigue, shortened patience, and always being in catch-up mode. Sleep is your success, so I want you to get in alignment with your bio-time and get consistent with it. I want you to utilize fifteen-minute adjustment increments in order to wake and sleep at your ideal times. Shift backwards every six days until you are living in alignment.

Are you a Bear that wakes at 7:30 a.m. when you should be waking at 7:00 a.m.? Then move it back to 7:15 and do this for a week, then shift back again. Are you a Wolf who goes to sleep at 1:00 a.m.? Move it back to 12:45 a.m. and do this for one week, then shift back again.

The Reset:

Back into your bio-times in fifteen-minute increments every six days until you've achieved alignment.

Now that you know what you are and what your ideal bedtime and wake times are, let's start adding what you will complete and when into the equation.

TWO: WORK BLOCKS & GOALS

You are most efficient when you block out your time. By blocking out like items within the same block of time, you will be more productive and proficient in specific tasks. What you do and when you do it is a powerful thing, and that is based on your bio-time to understand when you have the most energy for particularly demanding tasks.

Based upon your chronotype, here is your ideal work block segment. These are typically two- to three-hour segments (highlight your chronotype):

DOLPHIN

BRAINSTORM: MID-MORNING

Keep it light and fun: Get creative with your kids, plan business ideas or your day, read, or draw; this is a good time for laundry and household tasks too.

MEETINGS: EARLY AFTERNOON

Get to work: Call your family, have playdates, Zoom with clients; this is when you get active and out there with interaction.

DIFFICULT TASKS: LATE AFTERNOON

Use that brain: You have the most energy now, so do your most difficult objectives for the day, whether it's writing a blog post, crunching numbers, or helping tutor your kids, this is the time you have your full focus and brain power.

BEAR

DIFFICULT TASKS: MID-MORNING

Use that brain: You have the most energy now, so do your most difficult objectives for the day, whether it's writing a blog post, crunching numbers, or helping tutor your kids; this is the time you have your full focus and brain power.

MEETINGS: AFTERNOON

Get to work: Call your family, have playdates, Zoom with clients, this is when you get active and out there with interaction.

Keep it light and fun: Get creative with your kids, plan business ideas or reflect on your day, read, or draw; this is a good time for laundry and household tasks too.

LION

DIFFICULT TASKS: EARLY MORNING

Use that brain: You have the most energy now, so do your most difficult objectives for the day, whether it's writing a blog post, crunching numbers, or helping tutor your kids; this is the time you have your full focus and brain power.

MEETINGS: MID-MORNING

Get to work: Call your family, have playdates, Zoom with clients; this is when you get active and out there with interaction.

BRAINSTORM: AFTERNOON

Keep it light and fun: Get creative with your kids, plan business ideas or reflect and reassess on your day, read, or draw; this is a good time for laundry and household tasks too.

WOLF

BRAINSTORM: MID-MORNING

Keep it light and fun: Get creative with your kids, plan business ideas or your day, read, or draw; this is a good time for laundry and household tasks too.

DIFFICULT TASKS: AFTERNOON

Use that brain: You have the most energy now, so do your most difficult objectives for the day, whether it's writing a blog post, crunching numbers, or helping tutor your kids; this is the time you have your full focus and brain power.

MEETINGS: LATE AFTERNOON

Get to work: Call your family, have playdates, Zoom with clients; this is when you get active and out there with interaction.

All information on Chronotypes is found within The Power of When, by Michael Breus.

For moms with young children: Make sure you break up your blocks into twenty- to thirty-minute segments. Kids do best in small chunks of time, so you get your work done while they independently play and then you are present for them again!

PREP PERIOD

I force all of my clients in the morning to determine what must get done during the day. I call this my morning meeting (if my girls are involved) or my prep period. I highly recommend involving your children, because they like to know what's coming during the day too. This is where I grab my planner, stand while drinking my cup of coffee, and say, "What will I accomplish today?" I block it out and prep it, so it's ready for me to dive into when it's time. This takes only about ten to fifteen minutes, and already at the onset gives you the feeling of control over the day.

My Morning Prep Period Will Be: _____

Is it Wildly Important? It's crucial to tie in what you should be doing with when you should be doing it. I'm a huge fan of *The 4 Disciplines of Execution* by Chris McChesney, Sean Covey, and Jim Huling. In order to execute on anything within our lives, we need to ask ourselves is it wildly important? If it's not important, then why are you doing it? To appease someone else in a half-hearted attempt to do it all? Because you feel like you should? Shoulda, woulda, coulda are no longer in your vocabulary as a balanced boss babe.

Each time ask yourself, "Is this wildly important to me and will it guide me on where I want to go in life and who I am becoming?" If not, then it's time to say pass.

Value Check!

When deciding what you wish to spend your time on, I want you to go back and address those Top Five Values. How can you live them daily? Within the Resource titled "How I Live My Values Daily," I share how I structure and align my day with what's most important to me, leading to a passion-filled, simplistic life. To-dos aren't meant to fill your time, but fulfill a meaning.

THE POWER OF SIX

Fun Fact: My Anniversary is March 4, 2012, because 3 multiplied by 4 is 12 (yeah, I'm that kind of a nerd). I love math and use it to make my life so much simpler (and help my husband remember our anniversary date). I've done a lot of research on time management, and no one seems to have a good rule of thumb for how much we can realistically conquer in a day. Some articles said seven to ten tasks and others said one (they obviously didn't have children).

So, when I was reviewing my own clients' schedules and how they can be the best managers over their lives, I developed the Power of Six Model.

I want you focusing on 6 objectives each day:

3 large objectives

3 smaller objectives

12 hours in a day / 6 objectives = 2 hours per objective

This is still leaving you with 12 hours leftover to sleep, eat and rest

The weight you place upon an objective is up to you, and obviously a little task won't take two hours, but it shows you how much time you have to complete these six important objectives. The three bigger tasks I give greater weight to, so one objective may have three hours and another only one. All six objectives should equal twelve, however, so you balance your time.

Example: For those who have control and consistency over their health and fitness lifestyle, their workout may be a smaller objective, versus someone who is just starting their journey, which would make it a large objective. This takes time and effort to understand how and when you should structure, as well as the weight but is a good rule for you to live by and begin diving into.

BEAUTIFUL BALANCE & BOUNDARIES

If at the beginning of the Playbook you did not understand what balance meant, then you also probably do not understand what boundaries mean either. But, hey, this is your intentional transformation, and the journey of learning and growth towards becoming a mom boss.

THE TRUTH ABOUT BALANCE

Balance in itself within motherhood is unachievable. While the Power of Six allows you to handle a lot throughout your day, it doesn't mean that your life is perfectly balanced. Achieving balance means everything within your life has equal weight, and that's not how life works. If you are a career woman, you may feel like certain relationships are suffering. If you are a stay-at-home mom, you may feel you are missing your purpose and fulfillment. And if you are a work-at-home mom, you are just trying to get to the next naptime to get anything done. No matter what you do in this life and who you are, you will always feel the scales pulling in one direction versus another. This is why I want you to focus on leading a cross-balanced life.

"When you gamble with your time, you may be placing a bet you can't cover."

- Gary Keller

Don't gamble with your time, love, and energy. You most definitely will not feel balanced. Cross-balancing is the art of diving in, completing, and fully moving on. Life is filled with things that are undone, but if you cross-balance well, you are hitting your priorities and values and that's the most achievable thing we can hope for. That's your success.

Choose what matters most, the task at hand that requires your focus, and give it all your energy. Utilize work blocks and timers to define the period of work and once it's time to move onward, you close up in full for the time being (if it must be continued later) and cross over to the next task and role.

The Boundaries are the "Yeses" in Your Life. I want you to begin to think of boundaries in a whole different manner. Creating boundaries means saying yes to the most important things in your life that continue your intentional journey forward and saying no to the things that get in the way of that. So "no" more often means saying "yes" to only the right things.

Look at your life and write down what you should be saying no to. This is the beginning of development of boundaries and then we begin to delegate.

_____

_____

_____

_____

_____

DELEGATE

If you find yourself doing 394 things in a day, then it's time to utilize your asking muscles. You know, the words "Can you do this?" or "Can I ask for your help?" Yeah, those muscles. We cannot and should not do it all for everyone, so if you find yourself running on fumes and not following the Power of Six Model, then I recommend delegating efficiently. It doesn't make you weak, it makes you smart. And as intentional, unstoppable real moms, we all like to work smarter.

These are the things I would like to delegate and who can take them on:

Tasks	People Who Can Handle

FOCUS AND REST

As someone who is naturally all over the place all the time, focusing is a struggle because when I'm working on one thing, I'm thinking of another. Focusing on one specific task at one specific moment will get you to pause, fully dive in, and comprehend so you can finish and move on. Building in rest throughout your day will make you more productive during periods of work and focus. The harder the focus of the objective at the moment, the more rest and fun you need in order to replenish your focus muscles.

As I'm sitting here writing this, my timer is set to go off in ninety minutes (deep focusing period). After that, I'm going to do puzzles with Ava, have lunch, change over the sheets in the laundry, and just play for an hour, then back to writing!

SWITCH TASKING AND MULTITASKING ARE BIG FAT LIES

"You can do two things at once, but you can't focus effectively on two things at once."

- Gary Keller, The One Thing

Multitasking: The performance of more than one task at a time

Switch tasking: Doing multiple tasks that don't relate to the same outcome

Your prefrontal cortex (the focus epicenter) is the part of your brain that shines the spotlight on the task at hand. The prefrontal cortex can only fully direct its attention and focus on one task at a time, so in order to conquer the task to move on, focus on it fully in your designated work block.

We've been taught—since computers can succeed in this (I currently have fifteen tabs open)—that if we try hard enough, we can be multitasking and switch tasking bad asses. *And it's a BIG FAT lie.*

When you try to multitask, your brain is constantly being pulled in different focus directions, making you more inefficient and not able to fully close out what you are meant to be working on. Switch tasking also causes disruption in your workflow. Whenever you are interrupted to complete another task (like working on a spread-sheet and your kid says they're hungry for the 547th time that day), the distraction causes you to switch and have to reorient your mind before you can focus again.

This could be seconds or minutes, something of which us as moms don't have time to waste. *This is why you block your time out and focus on one thing at a time.*

If you have younger children, think smaller chunks of time for you to focus to minimize the interruptions. When my girls were four and two respectively, I utilized twenty-minute workflow windows, which allowed me to fully focus while I gave them a task to complete or an episode to watch.

Now depending upon your Chronotype, your work blocks will vary on what type of task to complete when. Make sure you go back to the Work Block section to understand what you should be doing and when. This means setting aside focus times based upon when you have the most amount of energy. This will guide you through to completion of your hardest objectives in the day.

THREE: TRANSITIONS AND TIMERS

Your lack of cues within your life is hindering your potential to be productive. Fun Fact: I'm a naturally lazy person—I think most of us are, to some extent—so in order to get done what I need to, I need to make it compelling and exciting, as well as reminding myself to do it. And with a jumbled mind and someone(s) pulling at you 24/7, those little, sometimes really important things get missed.

SET YOUR TIMER

This signifies what you will do when and a simple "hello, do this now," will send you moving. During your prep period, set your timers so you can stay in alignment with your daily planner so "nothing gets forgotten." Planning it out on your calendar will help you with WHAT you are supposed to be doing, the timer will cue you into WHEN. Set a timer, stick with it, and watch your productivity GROW.

TRANSITION AND FLOW

Your productivity is ultimately dependent upon how much you can get done in a short period of time, but also how effectively you close out the current task to wrap your mind around the next one and lessen your reorient period (the time it takes to refocus). This is where transitions are crucial, so you can close out your mind on the current task to open it up for the next one.

1. Stand up from seated position (if sitting) and stretch

2. Pull together all items you were working on

3. Talk about what you did (yes, out loud) and where you are finishing in this period of time

4. Make a note of where you left off if it's not complete

5. Organize items to close out

6. Put items back in home base (based on *Kick the Clutter*)

7. Grab planner to find out what's next

8. Move on

This is now your transition system; start implementing it so you can see your productivity grow.

FOUR: RULES & RITUALS

Rules and rituals help us establish consistency and order in our lives. If you are a free-spirited, hippie-type, then rules sound like the curfew that pisses you off. Trust me, I get it. I got rebellious for a period, too, but having rules and rituals for things that are important to you is your consistent reminder as well as your recipe for success in this life.

I love the philosophy "Don't break the chain," also known as the Seinfeld Method by Jerry Seinfeld. It's a mini-mantra to remind yourself to continue to show up, even when it's hardest. Consistency is queen, and not breaking the chain on your most important tasks and to-dos is the literal creation of rules and rituals for yourself and the stage of your success.

It's because of this that I stuck it out and finished this book that you're reading. It's because of this that I've accomplished so much in my business. It's because of this that I've created lasting, meaningful relationships. And it's because of this that I am healthy-ish (cookies are still my love language). My rules remind me to love the process, not just the progress attained.

Rules and rituals are reminders for us to stay accountable within our tasks and to-dos. A rule I have for myself is I MUST make my bed every day. Science shows that by making your bed, you are increasingly more productive throughout the day, plus it's an instant mood boost. So I always make my bed!

Another rule and ritual I want you to have for yourself is the Power Down Hour and what it entails. Make it meaningful and impactful. It's time for you to get spiritual AF with yourself and make your life one big ritual, or at least at the start and end of each day. Answer this Question: *What do I need to do in order to be the best me possible?* That's the beginning of rules and rituals for your life.

My rules for my life are:

_____

_____

_____

_____

FIVE: TRACK & CHECK

I'm not making you read all of this for shits and giggles, but rather helping you set the stage to elevate your whole life. It takes accountability. It takes consistency. And it also takes tracking and checking to ensure you are headed where you need to be going. Reflection is necessary for us to learn and grow. Reflecting on one's time and productivity helps us also become realistic with how much we are wasting. Did you spend two hours mindlessly scrolling through Facebook or Pinterest today? Yeah, that's what I mean.

I love the Goals & Habits Tracker through Tula XII, as it allows me to watch my goals be completed (or not). It also helps me realize as I compare it to my planner what I'm actually spending my time on. I also use the Undated Weekly Calendar Insert so I can set my time tracking based on my Chronotype (some people start their days early, okay!?). Get a Tula XII, you will thank me.

Remember: We all have 1,440 minutes in a day. Are you spending it on the wildly important? Find a method of tracking that keeps it compelling for you and makes it a scoreboard of the game of life that you desire to win at.

We no longer complete meaningless tasks for the sake of checking off another box, but rather live in alignment with our values and make sure we are putting them at the forefront of our daily living. Stephen Covey discusses this a lot in his book *The 7 Habits of Highly Effective People.* Those values you determined at the start of the Playbook are defining your path forward.

Your roles are the person you are within those values (mother, wife, employee, business owner, individual, etc.). From there, I want you to determine your goals in order to achieve living those values and assign tasks to take literal action on those goals.

VALUES - ROLES - GOALS - TASKS[6]

This is how I want you looking at your whole life and how you segment your time from now on. One step at a time, one day at a time, you can achieve this balance.

SEEKING SIMPLICITY

For some reason, we just love to make life complicated. I don't want you making time management and utilization of your time complicated, though. I want you to break down each one of these steps, fulfill them, integrate them into your life, and truly LIVE YOUR LIFE. What does simplicity mean to you? What do you desire out of this life and how do you think you will go about getting it? (Jot some notes and thoughts below.) Always going back to your values and letting it carve your path forward is how to go from hot mess to balanced and blessed.

---

[6] Covey, S. R. (2020). *The 7 Habits of Highly Effective People (30th Anniversary Edition)* (4th ed.). Simon & Schuster.

PART 4

Your Self-Care

Yeah, You Gotta Eat That, Stephanie

A RANT ABOUT TAKING CARE OF YOU

"When you put junk in, you'll get junk out…"

I'm going to step onto my soapbox for a minute, because, well, I can, and you bought my book, so you are pretty much my captive at this point in the game. But it is for your own good, trust me.

For the love of God, you have to take care of yourself, woman. Those three-day old clothes with coffee stains (and probably spit-up, too) and that greasy, messy bun ain't doing no one any favors (including your inner badass, opportunistic self).

Don't feel targeted, because at one point I was the woman above. I was a mess and until I realized how to step up and why I needed to step out of my self-induced, coma-like funk, I was never going to grow.

Why should we take care of ourselves? No, it isn't for our spouses and not even for our kids. It's for ourselves. Our physical health. Our mental health. Our spiritual health. Our emotional health. And while we all "say" self-care is important, none of us are doing anything in order to care for ourselves.

I ran the question, "Is Growth Selfish?" by my Daughter Diaries' followers recently, and every single woman said, "You can't take from an empty cup!" But when I investigated each of those who made this statement, ALL of these moms and women were on "E" big time and voiced it loud and proud on their social media spheres.

It's almost trendy and popular to be a "hot mess" nowadays, when, in all honesty, it should not be. Not because sometimes this isn't our reality, but because when we lower our expectations to the bare minimum, we become the bare minimum inadvertently.

But you aren't reading this book to be the bare minimum or a hot mess. You are reading this book to step into your most unstoppable self. So, in this Play, I'm going to tell you what you should be focusing on, how to focus on it, and how to make it a part of who you are. You aren't training for a marathon but your life, and it's important to look at health and fitness as a fine balance between your lasting quality of life today and tomorrow.

PHASE 1: BALANCED NUTRITION FOR A BADASS BABE

You can't out-train a bad diet; that's why it's important to not only be active but also integrate balanced nutrition into your life. We start with nutrition because we all already eat, so it's the easiest to make adjustments to.

I'm someone who thinks fad diets are freakin' stupid. Yeah, I said that, and I won't be taking it back. Why? Because literally eating meat and fat isn't sustainable, Stephanie. You know what is sustainable? A Balanced Diet.

WHAT'S A BALANCED DIET?

Protein, veggies, moderate fruits and fats, and minimal carbs each day creates a performance-based machine of a woman. And yes, you can occasionally have that ice cream. (Life is meant to be lived—I'm not a monster.)

Feeling deprived? Often that's because we have trained ourselves to desire instant gratification, and that chocolate cake at 8:00 p.m. sure tastes good. But limit what you indulge in, because it actually causes inflammation, sleeplessness, and a spike in your glucose levels.

START SMALL WITH SPECIFIC FOCUS

You aren't a fully transformed woman in one day. It takes many, many years to develop these habits, and it will take a few months of disciplined routine in order to kick them.

Pick something you want to focus on. Here's a list, but you can pick your own:

1. Track & limit your carbs

2. Implement a fasting routine and manage your calories

3. Reduce & eliminate sugar consumption

4. Focus on meal planning & prepping

Whatever your health and fitness goals are, you have to quantify them. When we track numbers, it's a lot easier to manage and adjust. So, pick one of the strategies and let's get going. As you'll see throughout the Playbook, Clarity is QUEEN, and quantifying your intake will help you understand what goes in.

A Smart System

What I won't be covering in this book is how our bodies process what we take in. I'm keeping this basic, but I do recommend the book *Eat Smarter* by Shawn Stevenson to understand how certain foods are processed within our bodies. For my own sake, I'm sticking with the numbers game.

TRACK & LIMIT YOUR CARBS

I'm a total nut for the Portion Fix system by Beachbody's Autumn Calabrese, because I literally shove my food in containers to monitor how much I eat. *Easy, make it easy.* This allows you to monitor how many carbs you are taking in, which is roughly one to two cups, depending on your caloric intake and plan (all based on your BMI).

IMPLEMENT AN INTERMITTENT FASTING ROUTINE AND MANAGE THE CALORIES

Our bodies do amazing things like ALL THE TIME. And it's even more amazing when we allow our bodies to kick our metabolism into gear. This is achieved when we aren't putting more in but allowing our bodies to use fat as fuel.

Intermittent fasting is cycling our eating windows and what is known as fasting periods (the time in which you aren't taking in any calories). There are many schools of thought and practice on how to burn fat most efficiently, but the tried-and-true method is 16/8: Sixteen hours of fasting followed by an eight-hour eating window. During that eight-hour window, try to maintain Portion Control to be most effective with your caloric intake.

REDUCE & ELIMINATE SUGAR CONSUMPTION

I'll be honest, this one hurts me to even include, because cake and cookies are my Love Language; however, sugar is killing us. It's killing your energy and making you irritable, so this is a great one to work on initially. because if you remove it from your house and create rules on what you can and cannot have, it's relatively easy to follow.

I did a detox where I removed all obvious sugars from my life. This did not include natural sugar from fruit or minor sugar found in some foods—those are harder to avoid—I did limit it though (like don't have five apples a day to get sugar). I focused on obvious sugars found in sweets, candy, coffee creamers, etc. I did a thirty-day sugar detox and while it was difficult, it made me realize how sick I felt when I ate a lot of sugar.

If you struggle with inflammation, coffee may be a contributing factor, so limit it and see. I know with my case—having endometriosis—it's a huge factor in my gut health, so test and see.

I'm just so sensitive...

I also recommend getting a food sensitivity test because not all bodies are built the same. While broccoli is perceived as good, it may not be great for your body; that's why it's important to gain clarity around what's right for you.

MAKE IT EASY

I'm literally on the path of least resistance, and nothing is more difficult than coming out of a three-hour conference call—starving and half brain-dead—and thinking rationally when it comes to what to cook for lunch or dinner. I recommend if you are living very much on-the-go, find a set of healthy recipes that allows for you to plan ahead and portion out, so you can grab-and-go, even if it's just right back to your office to continue working.

Pick a consistent day of the week to get groceries, transitional flow into prepping, and then put them away, so they're ready for you to grab when you need.

Did I eat today?

This has never been my problem because I think about food 25/8, but if you are someone who forgets to eat, then I recommend setting timers for yourself. This will help keep you consistently fed, minimizing the bad decisions you will make in an "extreme hunger zone." Plan it - Prep it - Time it - Eat it

HYDRATE YO'SELF!

We are literally a society of walking, dehydrated zombies on the average. We often mistake our thirst for hunger and think that the coffee we drink is providing us with enough H_2O to survive. *Wrong.*

I want to keep this super basic, and this is how much water you are going to start striving for every day:

Your Current Body Weight / 2 = Ounces to Drink Daily

This will help keep your skin clear, help you flush out your system, and just make you feel better.

———

Continue to build upon this. If you conquer one area of nutrition, it's time to find the next. Educate yourself on what's right for you. Seek a nutritionist that can guide you and help you live your healthiest life. And put your health at the forefront of your endeavors.

"Those who won't make time for their health will be forced to make time for their illness."

- Unknown

Make this transition as easy as possible. Get consistent with it. Make it obvious, so you know what to do and how to do it. Reward yourself for a job well done with something other than food.

PHASE 2: MOVING INTO BADASS BABE MODE

But I don't like being sweaty, Lisa. But I don't have time with the kids, Lisa. But I barely could afford this book, I can't afford a program or trainer, Lisa. I know, all of these excuses sound so nice and justified, but they aren't suiting you. Do something for me really quick, please. Write down your excuse for not having a fitness regimen and/or active lifestyle. Did you do that? Great. Now, mail it to—just kidding, I don't care about the excuse, and now neither will you.

Do one of the following with your excuse for not taking care of yourself: Shred it, light it on fire, stomp on it, tear it up. Whatever your means of destruction, make sure it's destroyed. (Just don't burn the house down, please, you just organized it.) Now, you can't use that excuse anymore. Now, we can focus on the way forward.

PART A: PICK YOUR ACTIVITY

I don't need to get into the benefits of fitness because we all know it's important and what it does for our well-being. I will state that maintaining an active lifestyle will increase your energy levels, level up your mood, lengthen your time here on earth, and increase the quality of that time.

The key here is training for an active and proactive lifestyle, where you get into a good regimen for your long-term health, not because you are ill and trying to compensate.

First, you need to pick the fitness program or activity you will be doing. I've been a Beachbody Coach for years now, and I completely understand that everyone has their likes and dislikes. I will say, however, that if you partake in an activity that can either incorporate the family and/or be done at home, you will be far likelier to succeed.

Let's take a moment and dive into YOU.

What are some activities I did as a kid that I enjoyed doing?

_____

_____

_____

If I thought of myself as an active person, what would I see myself doing?

_____

_____

_____

If it's fun, then it's easier. If it's easier, then it becomes a habit. Living an active lifestyle isn't about burning yourself out, but rather about enjoying the active things you do that grant you more energy and hopefully more time on this earth. Make the action of fitness easy, but the actual program has to be enough to show results. This isn't some walk-the-treadmill for an hour, Stephanie, and then fork down a Big Mac; it will have negated the work you've done, and that's inefficient.

For the outdoorsy moms, I recommend: hiking, biking, swimming, running/jogging, or walking with the stroller (extra resistance and it gets the kids out with you). Sometimes, just getting ourselves out of the house for a bit and changing the scenery lightens our mood and uplifts our spirits.

Mom Hack:

Load the kids up in the stroller with breakfast on-the-go. This occupies them, allows you to get your workout in and ensures you won't have to pick 500 pounds of crumbs off the kitchen floor post-breakfast (just dump the stroller out when they're done).

For the moms who prefer inside, I recommend: a fitness program platform like Beachbody, Peloton, or Zumba; they are all great. Seeking support from a community or accountability from a trainer will help solidify your habit. I know a lot of great Beachbody coaches that guide their clients through their journeys.

PART B: SCHEDULE IT IN

Consistency is Queen, so when you have that routine we talked about, determining when you will be active is important.

YOUR WHEN

Remember from the last Play, what and how is important but also the WHEN. You may need to slightly alter this due to your lifestyle, and that's okay, just get as close to the fitness window as you can!

Here are your ideal fitness times based upon your Chronotype:

Bear: Light walk before and after lunch; 6:00 – 7:00 p.m.

Before and after you eat, you need to get your body moving to start your digestive process, so a small walk (with the kids!) will help you get that digestion moving! This will also help you decrease your appetite and keep you energized to continue to chase the little monsters. In the evening, work out before you eat dinner, for this exact same reason.

Dolphin: 6:30 a.m. light exercise; 1:00 – 4:00 p.m. exercise window

In the morning, you will feel groggy, so release those endorphins and elevate that cortisol to help kick that sleep inertia. During your afternoon slump, get moving to help power you up for the evening. Get outside for a nice, long walk or jog, or play with the kids in the yard.

Lion: 5:00 – 6:00 p.m.

In the evening, Lions are exhausted from a full day, so boost that energy level with movement. This is dinnertime for some families, so just get as close as you can to your optimal fitness window to see the most benefits of optimized energy in the evenings. For me, we eat at 5:30 p.m., so I work out from 4:00 – 5:00 p.m. and still feel the same amazing benefits. Go for a run with the kiddos or lift some weights outside.

Wolf: 6:00 – 7:00 p.m.

You have the energy to actively engage, so now it's time to use it. This will help calm your busy mind by being intentionally active. Feed your kids and then run them to the park and let them play while you do laps—your dinner is when you get home!

All information on Chronotypes is found within The Power of When, by Michael Breus.

Utilizing not only your availability but your natural flow of energy will aid you in conquering this endeavor. The act of fitness itself won't be easy in order to see results, so making the process of fitting it in will help this be executed. Now is the time to turn back to the routine you've created and fill in and highlight where fitness will be scheduled.

Meeting with Myself...

Treat fitness like a meeting or appointment with yourself. You can't miss it without consequences. Those consequences are your health (which is, like, really freakin' important). Scheduling it in, getting the clothes on, and pushing through daily is tough, but so worth it once you see those benefits compound. Bonus points if you have to check in with your coach or accountability partner after—it helps with motivation.

PART C: ACTIVELY ENGAGE

You can't just show up and half-ass it. In order to elevate your heart rate to be healthier and see some results, you need to actively engage and push the boundaries on what you think you are capable of.

MAKE IT EASY, BUT ALSO HARD...

Make it easy to incorporate fitness into your lifestyle, but when you are showing up make it challenging on yourself to see results. If you push those five-pound weights up like nothing, go up to eight.

Do this by monitoring and tracking what you started with and how often you've increased the weight limits. Heavier weights make you work harder and therefore burn more calories and build strength. Also, track and monitor your speed, distance, and heart rate when getting outdoors. Are you going for a light walk that burns nothing or a brisk walk that gets your blood flowing? Be honest with yourself here. You have limited time to work out as it is—make it count.

PHASE 3: SUNNY D FOR THE BALANCED BABE

Well, Lisa, why include Vitamin D? We all know we need it. You do, do you? Well, considering how an estimated 1 billion people are Vitamin D deficient,* I think you kinda don't know how important it really is.

*Study conducted by the National Institute of Health in 2014

Why you need it: Vitamin D deficiency contributes to a huge multitude of health complications. Research conducted by the NCBI in 2014 has a table that shows what suffers when you are deficient:

TABLE 1.

Vitamin D deficiency and associated conditions[7]

Cardiovascular	Cardiovascular disease, aortic dilatation, orthostatic hypotension
Respiratory	Bronchiectasis, asthma, cystic fibrosis, bronchiolitis, obstructive sleep apnea
Gastrointestinal	Inflammatory bowel disease, chronic hepatitis, liver cirrhosis, pancreatitis
Neurological	Multiple sclerosis, myasthenia gravis, meningomyelocele, depression
Musculoskeletal	Muscle weakness, osteoarthritis, rheumatoid arthritis, juvenile arthritis
Metabolic	Metabolic syndrome, diabetes mellitus, diabetic nephropathy, infertility (male), chronic kidney disease
Cancer	Breast, colorectal, ovarian, lung, prostate
Skin	Psoriasis, systemic lupus erythematosus, eczema

HOW TO GET IT

If you live in a sunny place, go outside for fifteen to twenty minutes a day and bask in the sun. It's okay to do it in a small amount, and, actually, the benefits outweigh the risks. If you live somewhere where the sun isn't readily available, then I recommend adding Vitamin D into your supplement routine (see your doctor for the dosage) or incorporating foods with good sources of Vitamin D. Some foods high in Vitamin

---

[7] *Understanding vitamin D deficiency.* (2014, September 1). PubMed Central (PMC). https://www.ncbi.nlm.nih.gov/pmc/articles/PMC4143492/

D include salmon, red meat, egg yolk, raw maitake mushrooms, and orange juice (organic). Whatever means you get it in—ensure you are not deficient in Vitamin D.

PHASE 4: GET SOMEONE TO YELL AT AND WITH YOU

Oh, my favorite. Because the first two phases don't work unless you actually do it, amiright? Hire a trainer, enroll in Beachbody with an active coach, or pair up with a friend and become accountability partners to ensure you follow through. *You can also borrow my second-born, Mia; she's quite exceptional at yelling all the time.*

Remember how I said consistency is key? Well, you actually have to do it to be consistent, so pick someone who motivates and fuels you to actually fit it into your routine.

CREATE THE COMPELLING SCOREBOARD

The majority of us enjoy a little competition, but if you don't care to compete with others, then make it a game for yourself. Create a system to track your habits and utilize the "don't break the chain" philosophy I discussed earlier in order to guide and grow your habit.

PHASE 5: YOUR MENTAL HEALTH

Mental health is something that needs to be discussed because it's so prevalent in our society today. A study conducted by the CDC stated that one in ten women suffer from depression, and about one in eight suffer from postpartum depression. That's pretty high and honestly, I think it's even higher.[8]

Well, what can we do about it? We HAVE TO spend some time on ourselves. We have to dive into remembering WHO we are, WHAT we desire in life and HOW to fit it in. Our sanity depends upon it. Your mental health is just as important as your physical health, and so that's why I have included this.

Please Note: If you suffer from a serious mental illness, seek help and tell those you love. Going untreated when you need treatment is detrimental to everyone, including you. The world needs you—don't let your depressed mind tell you otherwise, and it's not weak to seek assistance. GET THE HELP.

---

[8] Division of Reproductive Health. (2020, May 14). *Depression Among Women | Depression | Reproductive Health | CDC.* Centers for Disease Control and Prevention. https://www.cdc.gov/reproductivehealth/depression/index.htm

How can we improve our mental state? Well, first off, I think reading this book is your start. You want to learn, grow, and improve your life and it shows. Secondly, how you speak to yourself dictates how you feel about yourself. Being emotionally abusive to oneself won't fix your "flaws," but only intensify them. Lastly, expressing gratitude for all we do have is also a great start to realizing all we have to be thankful for in this life.

Fun Fact: When I suffered from Postpartum Depression (PPD), I had no real reason to be sad, but I was sad nonetheless, and that made me feel even worse. Once I began looking at the glass half-full and started implementing the strategies I've talked about thus far, my mood and happiness improved. And it can for you too. But be kind to yourself. Seek support when you need it. And understand that sometimes being unhappy is part of the journey of life, warranted or otherwise.

Starve Your Demons, Fuel Your Fire

KICKING YOUR NEGATIVE SELF TO THE CURB AND STEPPING INTO YOU

"Our beliefs grant us the ability to accomplish what seems like the impossible..."

You know that Negative Nancy that lives in your head feeding you a bunch of B.S. about yourself? Yeah, she's a total bitch, and I'm going to teach you how to NOT listen to her. (Sorry, if your name is Nancy, this is nothing personal towards you. I just really like alliterations. I actually personally know a Nancy, and she's quite a lovely person. So sorry, girl).

Why do we constantly seem to fall into this flow of self-doubt and guilt trips? Is it in our nature as nurturers that when we don't meet our own falsified expectations, we are doomed for failure? I honestly don't know, but my friend and colleague, Alysia Lyons, wrote an amazing book on releasing your mom guilt. That is not my area of expertise, but that life coach has done the research, lived and released the guilt, and helped me in areas I didn't even know were a problem. You can find her book referenced at the back under Resources.

But I'm here to talk about you and your feelings towards yourself. Your relationship with your best self (or lack thereof). We are what we reiterate to ourselves, and if it's constantly negative, how much do you think you'll be able to accomplish in life?

Fun Fact: We think upwards of sixty thousand thoughts a day, and nearly 80% of them are negative. Yeah, we aren't doing ourselves any favors.

It's so easy to get caught up in the negativity and self-doubt, especially when as moms we fumble constantly. But that doesn't mean we are inadequate; it means we are on a journey that requires grace, patience, and understanding. We are superhuman sometimes but human most of the time, and what we tell ourselves on a daily basis determines how often that superhuman reignites.

HOW TO STARVE YOUR DEMONS

First off, you are stronger than you know. You are stronger than society gives you credit for. Society needs us to be less-than, so that it can tell us what we want and need, instead of us knowing that for ourselves. We are born warriors, and somewhere along the lines we forgot about that ourselves.

Anytime you begin to feel doubt or negative thoughts creep into your head, I want you to redirect and redirect HARD. Now, this doesn't mean blocking yourself out to constructive criticism or the lessons granted from learning from one's mistakes; it does, however, mean you need to stop constantly beating yourself up about them. There's no guide on life (although this book comes pretty damn close, not to toot my own horn), so we are all just learning from our journey and finding our groove.

Losing and then Abusing

I mentioned this prior, but Ava, my first born, wasn't even meant to be here. That's because I would have been having my child that I lost the time I got pregnant with her. One in four women lose a child, but it's still something that we don't talk about often enough.

I remember Valentine's Day 2015: I had to go in for my D&C, because my body just wasn't miscarrying my baby that had already passed away. It was a physical and emotional trauma that I hate seeing other mothers go through. And it made me resentful as hell. I resented myself for not being able to successfully carry that baby and emotionally abused myself for a period of time. "What did I do wrong?" "What's wrong with me?" "What could I have done differently?" And I began to resent others that became pregnant after me, and seeing their joy made my loss even more painful.

This Play is about teaching you to be kind to yourself, so when you experience loss, trauma, or heartache, you can persevere with dignity, grace, and resilience better than I did during that period in 2015. It's part of life to feel sad, but not to be cruel to ourselves and others for experiencing a loss out of our control. Remember that and learn from my mistake.

Redirecting means positioning yourself in the best mental place possible to continue to move yourself forward successfully, and within the next few pages, I will be guiding you on the ways to positively redirect your mind and thoughts towards your unstoppable self.

ACTIVATED AFFIRMATIONS

Affirmation: The action or process of affirming something or being affirmed.

We hear about affirmations all the time because they are an extremely effective tool in retraining our brain to think more positive thoughts.

"Those who believe they can move mountains, do. Those who believe they can't, cannot. Belief triggers the power to do."

- David J Schwartz

Translation: You are what you think you are. Now it's time to paint a positive picture of yourself, so that you can build the framework of a positive, peaceful, and content life. This is done through action and affirming the great things about yourself.

Here are ten Activated Affirmations to get you going. Each affirmation includes a daily action and then a reflection, because this closes the loop of our understanding and acceptance of our newfound positive belief. When we act and reflect, we re-train our minds to believe, reshaping those neural pathways towards a more positive you.

I want you to write these, read these, say them out loud, act them, and reflect on them daily. While it seems like a lot, most can take just three to five minutes, and I know that you can find that kind of time, even in your crammed day, (especially since now you are effectively blocking your day out based upon your Chronotype). If you want to keep all your thoughts in the Playbook, feel free to utilize the pages in the back to complete this segment.

AFFIRMATION THEME:

Adaptable - I can adapt to changing situations in my life.

Action - Spend ten minutes doing something outside your comfort zone. Relish in the fear and rise to the occasion. Adapt to your feelings and the changes you experience.

Reflection - How did forcing yourself to adapt make you feel? When challenges occurred, did you rise to them or fall? How could you improve next time?

Appreciative - I am appreciative of all that I am and all that I am becoming.

Action - Today call three people and express your appreciation to them. Tell them what you love about them, acknowledge a strength of theirs, and tell them thank you for being in your life.

Reflection - What was their reaction? How did you feel about yourself in expressing appreciation for someone else?

Balanced - I put time and energy equally within all areas of my life that are most important.

Action - Today I want you to write the five things that are most important to you, aka your values. (Go back to the beginning where you wrote them and rewrite them here). Then attach an action that you will enact to fulfill this value. When will you take action on each of these throughout the day to live in alignment?

Values   **Action**

_____   _____

_____   _____

_____   _____

_____   _____

Reflection - How do you think living in alignment will help with your self-fulfillment? Do you feel that you can achieve consistent balance by being intentional and blocking it out? Why or why not?

Beautiful - My soul is beautiful, and the world should experience it.

Action - Today write three things that make you beautiful inside and out. Ask your partner, children, or friends to list three when they think of you. Add them to your list.

Reflection - What did you find out about your inner and outer beauty through this action? Were there answers that surprised you?

Capable - I am a capable and strong woman who faces challenges head-on.

Action - Today attack something you've been putting off. Break the challenge down and tackle it a little at a time until you've conquered it or set the path forward towards achievement.

Reflection - How did accomplishing that task make you feel? In what ways can you continue to push the boundaries, making you even more capable as a woman and mother?

Disciplined - I understand what it takes to get what I want out of life. My discipline helps me conquer.

Action - Today I want you to create one tiny habit for yourself (the habit can take anywhere from three to seven minutes—think tiny but challenging). What will the behavior be, when will you take action on it each day, and what do you hope to gain out of it once it's become a consistent habit? Repeat for thirty days. (This can be stopping a bad habit or starting a good habit.)

Add it to your scoreboard (I recommend the Tula XII Goals & Habits Tracker) and check it off each day once complete.

Action: _____

Time: _____

Location of Action: _____

Goal: _____

Reflection - Each day you completed your habit, how did it make you feel? What did you begin to realize about yourself during this process? How can you compound this habit to add more value and importance into your life?

Energetic - I look at new challenges and experiences with energy and enthusiasm.

Action - Today when something challenging, stressful, or scary comes up, I want you to repeat "I can and I will." Pause and look at it as a solvable problem versus the end of the world. Change your tone and energy around the situation in order to become triumphant.

Reflection - How did changing your tone from pessimistic to positive about certain situations change the outcome of your day? How do you think continuing this trend will affect your emotional well-being? Keep repeating this action.

Faithful - I believe in myself and my ability to conquer challenges I create.

Action - Today be an active participant in your own life, do something for yourself, and acknowledge why you desire and deserve it, despite its challenge to complete. Try something you've never done before, you've been struggling with, or are unsure of. Have faith that it will turn out.

Reflection - How did you feel putting faith in yourself? Do you believe these feelings about yourself can amplify with practice?

Honest - I am true to myself as well as others.

Action - Spend ten minutes writing down something you've been holding yourself back on. Why have you been holding back? What is your fear? How do you feel you can conquer this challenge?

Reflection - Have you been truly honest with yourself in the past about the barriers you've put up? How do you think you can positively impact your life by facing them head-on and being honest with yourself?

Passionate - I inject love and energy into everything I do.

Action - Today, whether you are folding laundry, cooking dinner, or diving into a project that you've been putting off, put a smile on your face and find a way to make it more fun. Dance to put the laundry away. Sing while cooking. Cheer yourself on when you manage to check off the box of that thing you've been putting off. Be passionate about all aspects of your life, not just the fun ones, because you can make anything fun.

Reflection - How did your day go making everything passionate and fun? Do you think you'd enjoy life more doing this all the time?

It takes thirty days to begin to form a new system of a habit, so I recommend repeating these ten affirmations at least three times. Don't worry, repeating the same affirmations over will only reiterate your belief and understanding of them. Each action and reflection will pose a different reality and belief about yourself as you grow and better understand your desires in life.

BUILDING THIS HABIT

Start small when building habits. We like to go all-in and then we just end up burning ourselves out. So, I want you to focus on a specific time every single day, set a timer, and then practice. Living your affirmations seems awkward and rehearsed at first, until it becomes so ingrained in your life that you exude positivity.

Have your affirmation nearby and carry this Playbook with you, so no matter where you are when the timer goes off, you can repeat and reiterate. Personally, I like to start my day off right, and I have the list of affirmations for the month. I repeat them and then pause to think about them in each aspect of my life. This also helps me anchor it to something I do every day: Wake up and meditate.

Or maybe you want to close out your day with gratitude and anchor it to your nightly bedtime routine. Gratitude and appreciation for one's life is one huge step in intentional and fulfilled living. Earlier this evening, I was heating up my tea, dancing in the kitchen and then paused to think about how wonderful my life was. But I didn't always show appreciation for life the way I do now; it took practice, effort, and diligence toward becoming who I aspired to be: A positive and happy woman who loves and appreciates her life. And it takes time and practice to feel that way.

Positivity Post-Its

Place your words of affirmation in places you need it most. If you are struggling with losing weight, then place an affirmation on your pantry door: "I am worthy of the healthy lifestyle I desire."

Remember: You are what you think you are, so let's make it positive.

HOW TO FUEL YOUR FIRE

"Life isn't about finding yourself. Life is about creating yourself."

-George Bernard Shaw[9]

Everyone is great at something. You can be great at a lot of things, but there's always something that makes us super special and unique, a passion that sets our soul on fire and makes us feel truly alive. And now you are going to tap into it. You are going to step into unstoppable. You are going to fuel that fire because you've been starving those demons and no longer allow them to hold you back.

You've decluttered your home and mind. You've put systems into place to allow your life to be disciplined while gaining freedom. You are on the right track to living a healthier, balanced lifestyle. Now it's time to fuel your fire. This is what gets you jumping out of bed every morning, eager to conquer the day. This is what puts that smile on your face, allows you to face challenges head-on, and gets you thinking

---

[9] Keller, G. (2021). *One Thing. John* Murray Press Learning.

about the future. And not enough of us women ask ourselves if we showered today, much less are we pursuing what it is we desire in this life.

STEP 1 TO PURSUING YOUR PASSION: EXPLORE THE MEANING OF YOUR VALUES

"Tell me what you want, what you really, really want..."

Remember those top five values you explored in the beginning of the Playbook?

Those are the things I want you to learn to live by every single day. When we live within our values, we live fully aligned.

What do these values mean to you?

_____

_____

_____

Who are you as a person when you think of your values?

_____

_____

_____

How can you implement these in your daily life?

_____

_____

_____

Dive in deep with what each means to you.

To give you an example here are my Top Five Values:

1. Health

2. Family

3. Meaningful Work

4. Security & Comfort

5. Education & Growth

To me, each is completely intertwined but also distinctly different in my fulfillment of each.

Now we know what's most important to us and what it means to us, let's take it a step further.

STEP 2 TO PURSUING YOUR PASSION
RELATE YOUR VALUES TO YOUR SKILLS

We are all good at many things, and we are usually particularly good in at least one thing. I want you to spend fifteen to twenty minutes jotting down what you are good at and what you love.

My Vision Producer, Alisa Manjarrez from The Happy Cactus Club, had me do this Spider Exercise to determine my passions and this helps relate it to your skills. In the center of a blank paper, write your name and draw a circle around it (or you can do this below). Then all around that circle, draw lines coming off, like a spider (see where the name comes from—witty, huh?). Then I want you to start listing out every single thing you love to do, are good at, or that is important to you. Get creative and dive in. Ask your spouse, ask your kids, and if you did Activated Affirmation "Beautiful," then add those here, too!

Your Spider should look something like this (with your own thoughts):

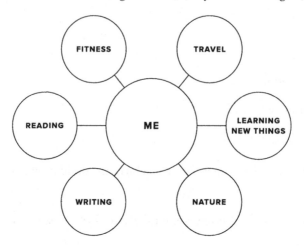

Then I want you to highlight in a bright and bold color the ones that are tangible skills. These are the things you could do on a consistent basis and see real movement in your life. Are you noticing anything about yourself through this exercise? Are there commonalities amongst the spider legs of skills, passions, and things that make you unique? Now it's time to take some action!

STEP 3 TO PURSUING YOUR PASSION: EXPAND ON THE THINGS YOU LOVE

From here, I want you to look at the big picture of yourself on this spider. This is your spider; give it a hug, nurture it, and say, "I'm a sexy spider." Okay, you can laugh, that is weird, but this is also you, and that's pretty damn sexy.

Next, I want you to pick something and expand on it. What action can you take to amplify this particular passion, skill, or thing you love? If it's creativity, I want you to get your hands dirty and be hands-on with something that sets your soul on fire. Fully immerse yourself in it, become fully focused on it, and see where it takes you. This is the art of exploration and further enhances that inner dialogue with ourselves, allowing us to be genuine and honest with who we are and who we wish to become.

Spend a month just exploring this and see what you find out about yourself. Spend ten minutes reflecting each night on what you explored about yourself and what you felt within the back of this book titled "Pursuing My Passion."

STEP 4 TO PURSUING YOUR PASSION:
THINK OF HOW IT CAN IMPACT OTHERS

From here, pick that favorite passion you explored and ask yourself, "How can this impact others in a positive way?" Research. Ask those around you. Drop the question on Facebook. Collect all the results and analyze them. What are you finding out about this passion? Can it be used in some form to help impact others either directly or indirectly in some way? Once we determine its impact on the world around us, that's when we can pursue it to grow and impact and potentially generate an income.

STEP 5 TO PURSUING YOUR PASSION:
GROW YOUR IMPACT / GROW YOUR INCOME

Focus on this one thing and go all in. What do you need to make this a reality? How can you take one step forward today? Who can you go to for support and assistance? Think BIG and get really specific on what you are going to do with this passion, who it will help and where you hope to go with it:

What I will do is: _____

Who it will help: _____

Where I hope to go with this big idea: _____

No matter what it turns out to become, it will be a lesson for you on focus and how you apply your energy. Start by starving those demons, then pursuing your passion will not only elevate your life but help you feel fulfilled, making you leap out of bed every single morning, excited to challenge the day. And that's really the meaning of life.

PART 5

Your Money

Why You're Broke AF

LIVING THE ABUNDANT LIFESTYLE YOUR WAY

"I understand what it takes to make my financial dreams happen..."

I'm going to make a bold statement and if you don't believe it, well, by the end of this chapter you will: Money is limitless and **you're** the one keeping yourself from more of it. True story. If you fall into the "deep shit" or "broke AF" category, that's okay; it's not the end of the world and you can pull yourself out with the proper education and resources.

Your thoughts and feelings regarding money play a huge part in your habits and behaviors around said money. If you hate and resent it, why would you want more to come into your life? (Psst, this is partly why you're broke AF.)

Okay, maybe you're not someone who is looking towards the horizon of bankruptcy. Maybe you're a mom making ends meet in a job you don't particularly like but pays the bills okay, and sometimes you can afford to get the Bacon Gouda along with your Venti Iced White Mocha (no whipped cream) during your Starbucks run. (That's my Starbucks order, if you feel inclined to get me one.)

This book, however, isn't about making ends meet; it's about stepping into your unstoppable self, becoming the badass that is hidden within, and leveling up your whole life. That means you need to get your finances figured out and invest in yourself for growth. Go for Growth!

HOW I KNOW WTF I'M TALKING ABOUT...

I love money. It started when I was three years old; my mom would frequently pull out her change, and we would discuss it, sort it, and I was allowed to do some chores to earn some of it. I was always asking my mom what I could do around the house to make some extra money, so she designed a weekly chore chart and assigned values to each chore. I was in charge of maintaining my activity, and pay day was on Fridays.

By the age of ten, I took my $800 accrued and opened my very first interest-bearing savings account at the local credit union. I built it up into the thousands over the coming years. Once I started college, I declared my major was business with an emphasis in finance and went on to graduate magna cum laude from California State University, Fresno in four years, which is really freakin' hard, by the way, in that timespan.

I've worked for a discount brokerage firm, a marketing firm in charge of operations and finance, and then went on to launch and manage not only three businesses of my own but nearly a dozen others for clients. So, I love money and I'm pretty sure it loves me, too. I live well and while we don't live in a mansion in Beverly Hills, we have the life we desire. (Note: We don't want to live in a mansion in Beverly Hills.) So really, this chapter, above all, is my expertise and education combined.

My husband, Matt, and I have been extremely blessed in our lives. We have a beautiful new home that we built; we both have college educations, have a nice car, two healthy and wild little girls, have been gifted opportunities that allow us to do what we love and make a living doing it, and have so many wonderful plans for the future that we are working toward today. This wasn't luck, magic, or the lottery that granted us this life, however.

It was smart, educated thinking about how to utilize money to the best of our abilities and make it work for us instead of working for it until we are dead. We aligned our most important values (that word again!) and set off executing them, one day at a time, one dollar at a time. But this book isn't about how awesome we are, it's about how amazing you're going to make yourself. So why are you broke AF?

There may be a couple of reasons you suffer from this complex:

LACK CLARITY

I was working with a client recently who had gotten into some pretty deep debt. When we started exploring how, she was amazed and didn't realize all that she was spending her money on; she lacked clarity.

When you don't know where your money needs to go or where it ends up, it disappears without a trace. This can lead to late payments, defaults that lead to collections, bankruptcy, foreclosure, you name it. If you don't budget for it, your money will disappear faster than it takes to order my Venti Iced White Mocha (no whipped cream). You may not intentionally default or overdraft, but when you don't have clarity around your money, its purpose, and where it's headed, this is often where it will lead.

LACK OF EDUCATION

When you don't understand how the system works with money and how to best utilize it to your advantage, that's when you feel broke AF. No, you don't need a four-year degree like me; you can seek advice from a professional or do your own research on generating active and passive income streams to aid in the longevity of your goals.

I developed Fit with Finances with my friend, colleague, and wealth adviser, Michael, to help individuals in aligning, educating on and implementing debt elimination techniques and growth strategies. There are great programs out there to educate yourself and resources that I've listed within Millionaire Mamas Club (my free community) for you to access and learn.

But if you don't understand and become knowledgeable about these resources and income-generating mechanisms, you will likely be living paycheck to paycheck for the rest of your days.

LACK WAGES

You may be broke AF if you live in a place you cannot afford and don't make enough to sustain the life you desire (or perceive you desire). You also may be broke AF if you just hardly make anything. Today's society is flipping expensive. From fresh produce and meat at the grocery store to the latest iPhone or the newest car with all those technological and safety features, to survive—and thrive—it often feels like you need to generate a million each month.

But don't worry; you don't have to become a doctor, lawyer, or corrupt politician in order to make ends meet. I will be guiding you later in the chapter on the ways to leverage what you have for growth.

YOU'RE SCARED AF OF IT

When you're terrified of something, do you try to bring more of it into your life? Hell, no. My fear of large bodies of water and sharks will always keep me beachside safe and sound versus diving in and boogieboarding. The same goes for money. If you resent it, are terrified of it, or push away opportunities due to indecisiveness, you are saying no to the opportunity (and money) that affords you the life you dreamed.

Money is a tool, a resource, and when utilized properly, money can actually grant you everything YOU desire in your life. It just takes a little understanding of your behavior, spending habits, and how to generate more of it.

THE MYTHS OF MONEY

I worked with my wealth adviser colleague, Michael, and we determined six myths about money and their truth-bearing counterparts. There's a lot more preconceived notions, but these are some of the common ones. These myths are believed by many, so we are here to set you straight.

Myths	Truths
Living paycheck to paycheck is acceptable	Living within your means towards growth is the way to live abundantly
Money is limited and evil	Your income, and how you leverage it, is the gateway to all your goals and dreams
Credit cards will lead to bankruptcy	Your misuse of credit cards will lead to bankruptcy; otherwise, they can be a great resource to leverage your potential

You need to start a retirement once you are in your career	You need to start a retirement with your first job and contribute via any means of income
Money management only matters when you make a lot of it	If you have $1, you need to manage it and assign it a role and purpose
Money can't buy happiness	Money is the means to help us become the person we were meant to be

MINDSET

This is one of the greatest components of your success (or demise). How you feel about money and were raised to think about it dictates whether it comes into your life freely or otherwise. Get your mindset right and the funds will begin flowing and you will become aligned.

Now is time to act and do some reflection. I want you to sit down and answer the following questions:

1. How were you raised to think about money?

_____

_____

_____

_____

2. What are your current thoughts about money?

_____

_____

_____

3. Do you find money evil or that it creates corruption?

_____

_____

_____

4. Do you find similarities in how you were raised to think about money and your current lifestyle?

_____

_____

_____

_____

5. Have you set yourself up to financially succeed or fail?

_____

_____

_____

_____

6. What defines happiness for you?

_____

_____

_____

_____

If you answered negatively in any of these, that's okay. Acknowledgement is the first step towards conquering. The last question is the most important because it dives into what it is that truly makes you happy. Everyone's definition of happiness is different, and below we will be assessing values to learn how to live aligned and content.

Once you learn to utilize money to its utmost benefit, you can leverage your potential to create the life you wish to create. That life looks different woman to woman, but the point is to open your mind to the possibility of welcoming as much money into your life as you need (while not needing money to be happy).

Hard Truth

Money is neither good nor evil; it's your potential to create the life you desire. If you hate or resent money, working on changing your thoughts and beliefs around it and diving into why you feel that way is crucial for your security and long-term success.

Are you in a job you currently hate, so the money you receive there you secretly resent?

Yes / No

Do you just wish you had more money, so you find yourself fearful of losing it when you receive some?

Yes / No

Is your current debt putting pressure on you, and you're feeling like you are drowning?

Yes / No

Were you not allowed to talk about money or financial status growing up?

Yes / No

And do you feel insecure about it?

Yes / No

Whatever the reason for the negativity, it's important to adjust it. And we adjust it by determining our values and lining up a budget that meets those values.

VALUES

Remember those values I had you determine in the very beginning of this book? Now it's time to bring them up again in relation to money. Doug Lennick, within his book *Financial Intelligence*, discusses the importance of developing a life around your values, and in turn, your finances and budgeting, accordingly, leaving you purposeful and self-fulfilled.

Time is money and your values are money. When you squander the two, you will find you are unhappy and unfulfilled and not understand why.

My Top Five Values (again):

1. _____

2. _____

3. _____

4. _____

5. _____

If you are married, then I recommend your spouse do this separately, and then come together and create a compromised couple's list. Why? Because not understanding what each of you want and then communicating it together is a huge reason why couples get divorced (aka your money and how each of you desires to spend it).

Now this does not mean that other things are not important to you, but it means that these are your top-focus, main priorities, and how you will align your budgeting and goals.

My Spouse's Top Five Values (1 being most important):

1. _____

2. _____

3. _____

4. _____

5. _____

Our Collective Top Five Values (1 being most important):

1. _____

2. _____

3. _____

4. _____

5. _____

Now that you understand what is most important to both of you, it's time to assess your current lifestyle around your values and then alter your budget for your values going forward.

YOUR CURRENT LIFESTYLE ASSESSMENT

Within *The Illusion of Money* by Kyle Cease, he asks the tough question: Are you living a life of 1s and 2s or 9s and 10s? This is in relation to the lifestyle you lead compared to those values that you determined.

It's time to go back to your values in order to do this exercise. Your values will fall within super important, (aka 9s and 10s)—if a particular debt doesn't fall within your values, then I would weigh it a 1, 2, or 3. Why? Seeing your spending habits laid out in plain sight will help you understand if you are living a meaningful life or one that society is trying to dictate to you. We all deserve to live a peaceful and calm life, and that means getting in alignment with our top priorities monetarily.

Helping You Understand the Exercise...

Bill: Kindle Membership

Value Alignment? 5th Value is Education

Assessment: 7

Explanation: Learning and growing is extremely important to me, so paying for a Kindle membership allows me to save money while I'm continuing to grow my knowledge through reading various materials daily. I ranked it a 7 because I don't have to have the membership, even though it is important, so if finances get tight, it can be removed.

Debt: Mortgage

Value Alignment? 4th Value is Safety/Security/Comfort

Assessment: 10

Explanation: My home is my safety and security, so making the mortgage payments (and a little extra when we can) helps me feel in alignment with a top value. I ranked it a 10 because it is a must within our family to have this home. It is non-negotiable in our eyes.

ACTIVITY:

1. Write down all of your debts

2. Assign a number to those debts based upon the values you determined above (1 being of not high importance; 10 being extremely important)

3. Ask yourself: Are you living a life of high value (9s and 10s) or of low value (1s and 2s)?

Debt/Bills	Amount ($)	Valuation

Help, What's a Debt?!

Debt is seen as a balance owed to someone or some institution. The car loan, your mortgage, student loans, and credit cards are all seen as debt. Your power and cable bills are seen as cyclical expenses and not necessarily debt (unless you don't pay them and a balance is carried). It's still important to add these expenses into your budget (see below) to ensure you remember to pay them.

Be critical about this. When looking at your phone payment, is technology and communication a huge value for you? If it is, then maybe having the newest, nicest phone IS important.

I did this one-on-one with a client recently and she asked me how does "peace"—one of her top values—equate to money? After I asked her some pointed questions, we began to understand that leading a simpler life financially free from her then-crippling debt is what she defined as peace.

Moral of the Story: Understand what those values mean to you in relation to your time (routine) AND money. It may take your life in a completely different direction. This is something we talk about continuously in Millionaire Mamas Club.

While money is limitless, we will never have enough if we try to chase EVERY materialistic thing. The point of this exercise is to find out if you are living a fulfilled life and determine how to make the adjustments necessary. This starts with a great budget and will lead to a truly abundant lifestyle.

BUDGETING

A budget is comprised of two components:

1. Income

2. Expenses

When you subtract expenses from the income, it should zero out or balance. Does that mean living paycheck to paycheck? No. It means you are allocating every single dollar to serve a purpose. When money is just "left over," it will get spent and usually on things of little importance (POOF!).

PAY YOURSELF FIRST

Within David Bach's book, *Smart Women Finish Rich*, he says that in order to grow

---

[10] Bach, D. (2018). *Smart Women Finish Rich, Expanded and Updated* (Expanded, Updated ed.). Currency.

yourself, your ultimate goal should be paying yourself first.[10] What that means is that you need to set up a brokerage account, savings, money market account, or some other savings mechanism that fits your needs and designate a specific amount of money to be automatically transferred into there each month. The reason for this is to create security and safety for your future needs and goals. You have to start planning today for the life you desire to have tomorrow, so setting the money aside first, will help keep your "extra" funds from going POOF.

Money goes towards your growth FIRST. I tell my clients and community that it needs to be for a purpose; align it with a value of yours to give it a use and something to strive for versus just aimlessly saving (that's not exciting). Within your budget, this is seen as an "expense" against your income, helping you "zero out" that balance sheet. This is the art of being purposeful with your money.

VALUE-BASED BUDGETING

You will now take those values and align them with a budget. This is easiest when you've categorized all of your expenses.

Your expense categories will include the following sections:

1. Housing

2. Utilities

3. Debts (Credit Cards, Student Loans, Auto Loans, etc.)

4. Transportation

5. Medical

6. Food

7. Personal Care

8. Savings / Investments

Ensure you allocate a portion of your budget towards those items that are most important to you. As time goes on, analyze where the majority of your spending goes so you understand your mindset, habits, and what adjustments you need to make. This is that clarity I was talking about earlier. The Objective: Live a fulfilled life without living for money.

RECONCILE OFTEN

Having clarity and control means understanding where your money is flowing, like I just discussed. This means picking one day a week (I call this Finance Friday) in order to input your expenses into your spreadsheet to see how far off you are on your budgeting goals. Feeling stressed about money? Find out where it's going.

DEBT ELIMINATION

If you are in crippling debt, you most definitely are not alone. Even our government is throwing out money like it's going out of style. But now it's time to put your big girl pants on, accept where you've gotten yourself, and then dig yourself out.

When procuring debt, the way to do it wisely is by buying yourself time or utilizing accounts with the least amount of interest. Utilizing cards with rewards points or no interest periods helps you to gain and leverage yourself when borrowing. If you have debt spread all over, then I would look into consolidating it for a better rate, buying yourself more time on payback, or having more control with it being in one place. I like to use a hybrid of two methods to get you going on your way to becoming debt conscious and controlled (debt is not necessarily a BAD thing when utilized properly).

First list out ALL of your debt. Then you will organize and utilize a specific method of elimination:

SNOWBALL

This means you start chiseling away your debt with the smallest balance first. Put your energy on that debt and then once paid off, move on to the next smallest until you eliminate it all.

AVALANCHE

Within this method, you will start with the greatest interest rate first. That means you are eliminating first the debt that grows the fastest. From there, work your way down until you have the smallest interest rate remaining and pay that off, too.

But Dave Says...

Yeah, I know Dave Ramsey says that debt is bad and you shouldn't have it. The reason is because he believes many cannot control themselves and will continue to get themselves into spiraling debt. But I'm here to tell you, you CAN and WILL be a big girl about your money and be in control of how you use it.

Truth: When you utilize debt as a mechanism of leveraging yourself for growth and you assess all your options for the best rate and timeline, then debt isn't the devil; it's a way for you to make the system work for you.

INVESTING

Now is the time to grow yourself. You've corrected your mindset and opened yourself up to opportunities, you've developed a budget that ensures you are paying yourself first and is based on your values, and you've now developed a debt elimination strategy to kick that debt to the curb. Now is the time to GROW, girl.

WAYS TO INVEST AND HOW TO GET GOING

I laugh because Michael uses this catchphrase every time I speak with him. This catchphrase is: "The name of the game is to get in the game." And he's 100% right. If you currently are not investing to leverage your income passively, then now is the day to start.

Another common myth that I didn't detail above is that people often believe they cannot afford a financial adviser. This is where most people are wrong because many financial advisers, like Michael, make their income on the growth of your income. So in turn, it's a win-win strategy.

If you wish to do it yourself, I recommend starting at Scottrade, where you can begin investing on your own. One caveat I will divulge is if you don't know what you are doing, then it's very easy to not invest properly and lose it. That's usually why I try to steer my clients towards a professional, because this is what they do 24/7.

There are a multitude of ways to begin investing, but even a simple brokerage account is a great way to start leveraging your money today. What is best for others may not be best for you, so I always recommend bringing your vision and goals to the pros in order to determine the best way to get going. This is often where a wealth adviser can tie in your goals with action.

I've included some questions for you to answer and take to them for your first meeting with Michael or any other amazing professional. Michael's information is in the back:

What is a lifestyle you hope to achieve monetarily?

_____

_____

_____

What are your short-term goals with your money? (1 – 5 years)

_____

_____

_____

What are your long-term goals with your money? (10+ years)

_____

_____

_____

When do you see yourself retiring?

_____

_____

_____

What do you plan to do in retirement?

_____

_____

_____

Don't worry—if you're broke AF there is a way out. Open your mindset to allow more money to flow into your life. Be purposeful with your spending. Pick a debt elimination strategy. Align your budget with your goals. Reconcile weekly. Oh, and lastly, get in touch with a professional, so you can grow strategically.

PART 6

Your Boundaries

Pivot Real Good

WHEN SHIT HITS THE FAN

"Shit will always hit the fan. It's our response
and readjustment that keeps us going..."

Yes, this is a play on the song "Push it Real Good" by Salt-N-Pepa. I'm an '80s baby—it's just in me. This Play is all about the reset, you know, when you've fallen off the bandwagon and need to get back on the ride (aka your life).

If you played Oregon Trail back in the day, then let's be real: you were the one that got bit by a snake and had to be buried along the way, all because you couldn't manage when shit hit the fan. But not anymore, girl! If you currently classify yourself as a hot mess with a double shot of express, then that's okay; that's the reason you picked up this book or it was discreetly gifted to you.

THE STRUGGLE IS REAL...

One time during a one-on-one with one of my favorite clients, she said she struggled with maintaining consistent flow in her daily living. She said she felt like her life was a rollercoaster of successes and failures. And this is completely normal. Between hormone fluctuations and inconsistencies with sleep and self-care, being on-point all the time often isn't a realistic expectation. Everyone falls off sometimes and struggles maintaining their mojo, so I've listed a few tips that I personally use and share with my clients on how to get back into it and shoot for 85% badass with 15% chaos management.

This is called your reset (you've heard this once before in the Routine Part). There are things in your life that will always need to be addressed, and small, specific action steps will get you there on a more consistent basis.

Please Note: If you've kicked the clutter already, it's a lot easier to stay on-point consistently. Trust me on this.

THE AREAS OF STRUGGLE

SLEEP

"What's sleep?" is a question I always get jokingly asked in my coaching calls. I know, I know, especially if you are in the phase of life with young children, sleep can seem almost nonexistent. The problem is that when we don't receive the adequate amount of sleep, our focus, productivity, patience, and overall happiness ultimately decline. So, unfortunately, this wasn't a "suck it up, Buttercup," moment for you on losing sleep. You're going to have to get more of it. We will be discussing this within the Reset Section shortly.

SELF-CARE

Our mental and physical health are often the last things on our mind when they should be our first. If we don't love ourselves, how can we love others? If we don't care for our bodies, what example are we setting AND will our bodies last for those who need us? This is one area you cannot compromise on, but it's also one of the hardest to maintain with so many other roles and obligations. Within the Reset Section, we will discuss how to start small again and build that habit consistently.

RELATIONSHIPS

We aren't even taking care of ourselves, so how can we foster strong, committed relationships? But the point of life is to find those to share it with. If we did this whole thing alone, it wouldn't mean the same. So, ensuring within our Reset that we find time to cultivate our most important relationships is the difference between a task-oriented life and a fulfilled life.

HOW TO RESET

Take a deep breath and ask yourself these important questions:

1. What is currently the issue?

2. What are possible solutions to the chaos that is currently being presented?

3. Is there a need to reset?

When we take a moment just to calm the storm, we start to gain clarity about the opportunities before us. So often as women, we just react to the situations and demands before us instead of pausing and saying, "is this necessary" or, "am I just filling my time?"

Calm the Storm

When it's just a total shitshow around here, I make us all take a timeout in the form of breathing. I force us all on the floor in the middle of the room, sitting down in the cross-legged position, eyes closed, and breathing in our noses and out our mouths for two to five minutes.

NARROW YOUR FOCUS

Just stop focusing on everything for a minute. It's pulling your productivity in so many directions that you can't focus on one thing, much less twenty-five things. I love Gary Keller's prompt within *The One Thing*, with what he calls the focus question. The Focus Question says: "What's the ONE THING I can do such that by doing it everything else will be easier or unnecessary?"

We want to look at the BIG picture but have a very narrow focus because as moms we struggle focusing for too long on one thing, regardless of immediate distractions. Think BIG, act small. Once you have this big picture—the end in mind—it's a lot easier to determine what the right things we should be doing are. Make sure you go back to Routine Queen (Part 3) and revisit the Power of Six Method.

"OMFG Lisa, not this whole thing again." Yes, Michelle, sleep is important, and you need it. Go back to Routine Queen (Part 3) and restart your Chronotype scheduling.

The Reset:

Back into your bio-time in fifteen-minute increments every six days until you've achieved alignment.

START SMALL WITH SELF-CARE

Answer these questions:

What does self-care mean to me?

What would these acts of self-care in my daily life look like?

Whether you pick up a book five minutes a day or are actively dancing in the kitchen while you cook dinner, life and caring for yourself is meant to be fun! You aren't training for a Tough Mudder (maybe you are, and I'm here to tell you it's hard as shit); you are training for a healthy, balanced, and fulfilled life.

Begin with just five minutes and then build. Habit formation, according to James Clear, author of *Atomic Habits*, is developed through practice, and making it easy to implement will make you successful in the long-term.

AUTOMATE & ANCHOR

Let's make life as easy as possible, shall we? That's achieved by placing things in our day next to other things we already do as well as making these actions automatic. Your hope is to eventually achieve what James Clear talks about as automaticity: The ability to perform a behavior without thought, when the unconscious mind takes over and does its thing.[11]

As moms, we have to think a million thoughts a day and provide dozens (feels like hundreds) of actions. Any extra things we can automate—like laundry or taking out the trash, or even showing up for your workout—will help alleviate the tension and overwhelm in your life.

This decreases your resistance and unwillingness to achieve hard things. Do this by scheduling it into your day and setting timers to remind yourself, slowly building that muscle memory. The more you do something, the more your body remembers.

Anchor the act of what you need to be doing for yourself with something you already do. My fitness block is right before dinner (ideal for my Lion Chronotype). I eat at a consistent time, so it made sense for me to anchor to it. Make self-care a part of your life and you will be thanking yourself.

GROW MEANINGFUL RELATIONSHIPS

First off, you cannot be everything for everyone, so stop trying to set fire to the relationship with yourself. You can, however, have close and meaningful relationships and good boundaries with those you love most (including yourself, remember).

Connecting with people will help give us that momentum towards seizing the day and embracing the moments within our life. By nature, we are social creatures (even you introverts), so establish how you see the relationship growing and developing by reaching out and maintaining contact.

FRIENDSHIPS & EXTENDED FAMILY

Make a list of everyone in your life, family and friends, that have meaning in your life. Living in alignment means connecting with these people on a regular or semi-regular basis. It could mean a texting conversation, phone call, or Zoom, or even a lunch date. Set the boundaries on the availability you have, but reach out to initiate and foster growth within the relationship. Who are you connecting with this week and how?

YOUR MARRIAGE

You know that person you sleep next to or pass by in the hallway just about every day? Yeah, that's your spouse, and you probably need to foster some sense of communication and connection with them in order to grow and continue your relationship. That means devoting time every single day to connect and communicate with your partner in some form or another.

Sadly, my husband, Matt, gets me at the last moments of the day, but that hour is just ours and no one (not even kids who keep sneaking in fighting sleep) can take that away from us. I'm not a marriage expert, but I have a great colleague, Megan Kirby, who helps guide women on their own personal journey through communication and connection with the love of your life. I'm including her contact information in the back of the book and where to find her.

CHILDREN

We know we need to give love and attention to our children, but there's a big difference between quality and quantity. I'm with my girls nearly all day, every single day as a work-at-home and homeschooling mom, and that meant I didn't feel the need for quality time. But I was wrong.

They are one of my top values, the people I love most, so each day they get individual quality attention just with me, so our relationship can grow together. We should never take them being around for granted, because someday they will leave home and then we will wish we had more quantity of time. So, embrace the quality. Pick an activity, lean into your children's interests, and connect with them.

YOURSELF

Sadly, I'm putting her dead last again, but not for the obvious reasons. I am putting her last in this section because I want this to resonate with you the most. You know you need to spend time with those you love, but you most definitely need to be spending time with yourself daily.

This Playbook has a lot of action within it, but the greatest action of all is having that inner dialogue with yourself. This is also one of the huge reasons I included so many pages at the back to write it out.

Even though this Playbook is almost done, don't lose sight of the importance of asking the questions towards your growth and why you matter in this life. Write to yourself daily and don't ever stop.

STOP THE MINDLESS SCROLLING

You know that thing you are constantly holding and mindlessly scrolling through about 90% of your day? Yeah, during a Reset, you need to set timers with yourself and be committed to removing social media and other time wasters in your life. Living a life around technology means other areas are suffering like our relationships and self-care, so while we live in a society dictated by social media, mitigate it for your health, well-being, and sanity.

Set a timer to alert you when it's time to get on and off, and follow this system to a T. This will allow you to have more time and clarity around the more important things in life.

And yes, for me, social media is my business and life, so I, too, have to make sure I follow my system of checking and engaging, but trust me, the other areas of your life demand it!

GET BACK TO THE BASICS

Remove anything else that isn't essential. This means that things within the whirlwind like feeding your kids will stay, but other unnecessary things will be put on the back burner until you get your schedule realigned once more and can add more. What's crucial for you to accomplish? Sometimes we need to go to the bare minimum in order to build that momentum again.

ACTIVITY:

Make a list with two columns:

1. Must-do

2. Hope-to-do

Within the Must-dos, you MUST put self-care time. You decide the self-care action, whether it's physical exertion, reading, journaling, napping, whatever, but put it into the must-do column.

Relate this to the Power of Six Model we discussed in the Time Segment so that your list looks simple and achievable. This should also relate to your values because those will always come first within your life.

MUST-DO   ## HOPE-TO-DO

_____   _____

_____   _____

_____   _____

_____   _____

_____   _____

_____   _____

In the words of James Clear, we must "start by focusing on who we wish to become," and everything will slowly fall into place. Start with the small and build upward. We are often too quick to fully dive in, causing us to repeatedly burn ourselves out. And remember: What's first in your life (your values) always comes first.

Zone Defense on Anxiety

FEAR MINDSET AND MENTAL HEALTH

"Once we know what we are capable of, our fear can no longer hold us back..."

(This was discussed in a previous Play, but needs to be reiterated and expanded upon.)

It seems like everyone I know nowadays struggles with the term, "anxiety." I get it, don't get me wrong, because I live in a Category 5 Meltdown Mode about 85% of my life. I'm a ball of stress, a worrywart, and someone who processes every scenario before it occurs.

Here's the difference, though: You cannot let it hold you back from your true potential. Stop being so scared you're stalling your life. You may have read this book and are scared shitless on where you are going to go with your life. Why? Because you don't know who is on the other side of this transformation. And that's scary AF, I know.

Fear, anxiety, and overwhelm are your mind's responses in order to get you to stop, halt, and not proceed forward. These triggers are created for your survival, but completely fight your ability to thrive.

"Greatness comes from fear. Fear can either shut us down and we go home, or we fight through it."

-*Lionel Richie*

You will feel fear stepping out of your comfort zone. You will feel anxiety saying goodbye to your past self. You will feel stress completing the arduous tasks it takes to transform.

I want you to assess how you feel right at this very moment.

Right now, I am feeling:

"My God, this woman is insane, I can't believe I've read this far into her book." Normal response, I get it, but keep pushing forward. If you are feeling stress, pressure, overwhelm, USE IT. Let yourself feel all the things, but move forward anyway.

Fun Fact: When you push through fear and accomplish the thing that would otherwise paralyze you, your body releases oxytocin. Yes, the love and happiness hormone. Akshay Nanavati, author of *Fearvana*, did extensive research into how the human brain functions when exposed to fear. Once you pass that threshold of fear and move through it, you experience what he's coined as *Fearvana*.[12] True and utter bliss.

Have you ever done something you were scared of and then felt so damn proud of after? That euphoria is Fearvana. At just four years old, my daughter, Ava, experienced it when we decided to climb rocks at the beach. The hill was rather steep, and she did not want to do it. My husband, Matt, and I urged her anyway and she pushed through. Still months later she was talking about how proud of herself she was. That's Fearvana.

---

[12] Nanavati, A. (2017). *FEARVANA: The Revolutionary Science of How to Turn Fear into Health, Wealth and Happiness.* Morgan James Publishing.

I didn't really realize the person I would become until the year 2020. I like to create a theme or a mantra each year and my theme for that year was "scare myself daily." I didn't know where I wanted to go with The Daughter Diaries, Inc., and so I decided to push myself out of my comfort zone to see what I was made of.

Little did I know, the whole world would completely shut down and pause, giving me time to really analyze what was meant for me. It was a pivotal moment in my life and one that is so grounding that I will never forget it. In those first few weeks of shutdown, my purpose and understanding of what my mission really meant to me revealed itself.

I led with my heart and gave my time, energy, and love. I offered free coaching, I put myself out into the social media world and helped women I didn't know. I was scared of what people would think of me, but I proceeded forward anyway. I was unsure what my peers, family, and friends would think about the actions I was taking, but I proceeded forward anyway.

I scared myself over and over until I became so crystal clear on my path forward, so damn laser-focused, that now nothing and no one can stop me. My fear was my fuel, and I used it over and over again to experience Fearvana and the action that even propelled me to write this book. That true euphoria I experience when I push past a challenge or I surprise myself is all I need to continue me forward. And now it's your turn.

Experiencing a rush by pushing past fear doesn't mean you need to go skydiving or do something else dangerous; but allow yourself to experience anxiety and fear over the unknown and push through anyway. So, in other words, anxiety is your pal, if you let it push you forward into greatness. Stop scaring yourself into stalling and step through your fears towards greatness.

Ditch the Bitches

FINDING YOUR TRUE FRIENDS AND SAYING NO TO MEAN MOMS

"Life is better with your Tribe…"

I think people are inherently good. I wholeheartedly believe this. But certain circumstances, experiences, and beliefs shape some individuals to be in the wrong places, with the wrong people, and get caught up in the wrong things, including gossiping about individuals who aren't around and cannot stand up for themselves or belittling those in their presence to compensate for their own insecurities.

True story: I was in a Mean Moms Club. This is true, I said it. I wasn't the instigator of gossip, but I definitely was the brunt of the negativity when it came to my first child, Ava, and me. I was different from them, and it definitely showed. Sadly, I held on for years thinking they were my friends. I just figured it was normal to be treated this way. I grew up in a small school system and a tiny town, so I just dealt with it—and I'm from the generation of Mean Girls—until I realized it wasn't normal or acceptable.

And it really came to light once my daughter was born. They'd make the most off-the-wall, rude comments about her and compared her to their children.

Sidebar: If you don't know my daughter, Ava, then you really should get to know her. She is such a special individual that was graced with both empathy and sympathy in her nature and is a bright light to those around her (she is, like, way nicer than me). She feels what others feel and attempts to process life way beyond her years. So, she most definitely is not inferior or deserves to be compared to in a negative way, just how I'm sure you feel about your children.

I won't get into too many details because negativity and belittling isn't the point of this Playbook, it's to make you the best version of you. But I had finally decided enough was enough and I began politely declining invitations with them, making excuses of why I couldn't attend that day. Until one day I just wasn't invited anymore. And as odd as this sounds, it hurt.

Why did I care if they were still getting together without me? I didn't want to be in that environment anyway—my husband even pointed out how horrible my mood was every time I left their meetups. But whenever I'd see them post about their playdates, I would be offended that I wasn't included.

By nature, we are social creatures (even introverts want to be invited). We desire and long to be accepted. We crave to be liked and included. And when we aren't, it stings. But I didn't want to go back to them, and I shouldn't. They weren't my people. So, I set out to find my people, find the ones that were there for me, loved my daughters, and rooted us on when they had no reason to.

In order to live this new me set on positivity and growth, I developed a few commandments, some rules to live by, and the reasons I would live them for myself and my girls. I am teaching my daughters the way to be treated and how to treat others, so this all starts with me and who is in my sphere of influence.

Please Note: I'm no relationship or life expert by any means. I do know, though, if you are in a bad relationship with people who don't share the same values as you or aren't good to you, it can be detrimental to your own well-being. So, find your people!

Here are the commandments to live by when you are exiting a Mean Moms Club, ditching the bitches, and setting out to find your people. If you, too, are in a Mean Moms Club, it's time to get out cold turkey. If you were or are the mean mom at one point, it's time to change. Spoiler alert: You and your children aren't any more special than their kids, so cut the crap.

Now is the time to find good people, be good people; the world needs us, as mothers and as nurturers, educators, and guides to be the BEST people, now more than ever in this broken world.

THE COMMANDMENTS

The Principles to Live By

COMMANDMENT 1: I WILL ACCEPT WHAT I CANNOT CHANGE.

Not everyone will do things the way I do them, and that's okay. Instead of comparing myself and my children to someone else and her children, I will accept we are different people and move on. I won't try to change them to make myself feel better. I won't argue with them for the sake of arguing. I will accept what I cannot change and move onward. What's that saying? It's not my circus, not my monkeys. Yeah, that one. I'll work on raising my little monkeys the best I can and let the differences be.

COMMANDMENT 2: I WILL SEE THE BEST IN PEOPLE.

Just because people differ from me doesn't make them bad. I will make a conscious effort to see the best in an individual. (I even did this with the women of the group I left, and it helped me to move on easier.) I will make a note of the good things about the women I meet, and I will choose to see them in the best light I can. If I make up my mind that they are not my people and don't hold the same values as me, then I can leave at any time—nothing is keeping me there—and continue to search.

COMMANDMENT 3: I WILL SEE THE BEST IN MYSELF AND LET IT SHINE FOR OTHERS.

In order to love others, I must first love myself. I know I have wonderful things about me, so I need to let it shine to the outside world. If I'm not appreciated for the things that make me good and kind, I will continue to seek out people that notice these things about me. I will not hide the best in myself—as the world needs more of it—and will continue to shine outward.

COMMANDMENT 4: I WILL MAKE SURE MY VALUES COMPLIMENT THOSE THAT I BRING INTO MY SPHERE OF INFLUENCE.

Just because people see things differently doesn't mean we don't hold the same values. Those that I bring into my sphere of influence I want to value or compliment mine. I will no longer try to uphold a standard outside of my values. I won't try to become someone who I wouldn't be proud to be.

COMMANDMENT 5: I WILL LIVE WITH PURPOSE.

No matter who sees it, I will live my life with purpose. It doesn't matter if others do not believe in what I am offering to the world; it is my purpose to fulfill, not theirs. I will seek out people who believe in what I am trying to accomplish, cheer me on, and support me in whatever way they can. I will help and aid them in their purpose, as well.

COMMANDMENT 6: I WILL SMILE AND BE KIND.

Whoever I come into contact with, I will always smile and be kind. I never know what battle others may be facing, and their actions may reflect the people they do not wish to be. So, no matter what goes on, I will always smile and be kind. I will be the best person I can be, and their thoughts, feelings, and actions won't interrupt my own well-being.

———

No matter who you are or what season you may be in, live by these commandments (and others you create for yourself) in order to be the best person you can be. *Remember:* No mean moms around here! Ditch the bitches, change your attitude, and be the best woman you are meant to be. The world needs it, your kids need it, and you need it.

PART 7

Your Win

Becoming a Balanced Boss Babe

You've made it this far. Congrats, I'm super proud of you. It's not easy finding the time to read this, much less implement the strategies within, but if you do, you'll find yourself with not only more time on your hands, but more patience, appreciation, and the feeling of being balanced and blessed.

You will also begin to view life a little differently. You will relish challenges and seek opportunities. You won't look at fear as a roadblock but an obstacle to conquer. You will notice the little things that life is here to show us, versus just letting life pass you by.

I HOPE YOU NOW FEEL LIKE YOU LIVE THIS LIFE: BALANCED BOSS BABE

This is what each mother is working towards, and what all the beautiful steps within this Playbook ultimately lead to. A balanced boss babe knows what she wants, how to get it, and the meaning behind everything she does (even if at that moment she's a snack bitch).

Life is meant to be lived, and the fear we feel when stepping into the unknown is meant to help propel us forward versus keeping us stagnant. If you haven't dived into these steps, that's okay; now is your time to take that leap of faith and get going, one Play at a time. Conquer it, add value to your life, and proceed onward.

Keep this Playbook on hand; this is your guide, your reminder, and your support system. Anytime you feel lost or need to find yourself again, pick up the Playbook to seek your answers—they are always hidden within. Your head. Your heart. Your home. These are the things we've been conquering on this journey together.

I'm not done quite yet, though. There's a few other topics that I wanted to string together so you could see the connection and make it all align perfectly.

Remember: This transformation is intentional, so we act and lead with intention.

AUTOMATION

It's time to assess your life and continue to look for ways to make your home, work, and life in general work smarter, not harder. Get aspects of your life to flow and work for you versus always in resistance.

Life is meant to be hard. But along the journey of chaos within motherhood, we step into our successful selves at the next level anytime we can find a way to level up and work smarter. Automate the difficult things within your life and reap the rewards.

AFFIRMATIONS

Never stop affirming your beliefs and believing yourself to be the best you possible. You are the woman your children need; be good to her. Consistently have that inner dialogue with yourself to further the love and appreciation and relationship with yourself.

ACTION

It's so easy within motherhood to feel like we will crumble, but remember always on the other side of action is how you will rise into your best self. A step forward is always better than just standing still.

FAITH & FEAR

You will always have fear when it comes to the unknown, but having far more faith in yourself is what it takes to rise up to any occasion or obstacle you face. Have faith and live with fear—and continue forward anyway.

TRIBE

Find your people. Embrace your people. Appreciate your people. Invest in your people. I would personally like to invite you to my Tribe, the Mamas Unstoppable Tribe, where we will continue this journey every day of our lives with the support of amazing women and mothers who desire to live life a little differently.

If you've done the Plays in this book, you see how much more calm, control, and clarity you have in this life, so now it's time to take yourself to the next level with women who support you and look forward to seeing you continue to grow. Find your Tribe, a place to be authentically you while elevating yourself with purpose and intention.

I really hope you enjoyed this book and didn't find me too bitchy. In all honesty, you have everything already inside of you to be totally badass; I just gave you the steps to execute it.

My goal is to change a million women's lives. That means if you've found this book helpful in any way, share it, so we can rise up together. I hope my book can be the start of a better world for us and future generations.

I would love to hear your thoughts and your story.

Here's how to reach me:

Email: info@thedaughterdiary.com

Website: thedaughterdiary.com

Access the free community, Millionaire Mamas Club at: thedaughterdiary.com/services/mmc

Join the Mamas Unstoppable Tribe at: thedaughterdiary.com/services/tribe

About the Author

Photography by Lirio

When all of Lisa's worlds collided and she became a mom of two little girls, she knew she needed to help other mothers find their place, their peace, and their passion. Her journey as an author started back when she was three years old. She wrote her first book about Mickey and his puppy (spoiler: his cat ate his fish, and so he ended up with a puppy). From there, she wrote in elementary and high school, and was published a few times for her creative writing and poems.

Once Lisa started college, she chose to pursue her degree in business with an emphasis in finance and entrepreneurship and began to hone her skills for time management and system creation. She graduated high honors and worked for several years at a local successful marketing firm, running operations, handling accounts, and managing production with a team of almost a dozen designers (total chaos). There, she learned the ins and outs of running a business and creating brands.

Lisa always knew in her heart that she was an entrepreneur, so after a few years in the corporate world, she set off and became her own boss. It was the most liberating and educating experience in her life (next to motherhood).

Since then, she has launched three of her own businesses, helped dozens of women get their life in order, had two little girls, became a Consultant via the KonMari Method™, and has one successful marriage to her high school sweetheart and football stud who supports every endeavor she has.

The COVID-19 pandemic made Lisa realize a lot of things: That life is too short to wait for the "right moment," that other mothers needed her interesting skills and considerable expertise, and that she—with the help of technology—could meet and guide amazing women all over the world towards becoming their best selves.

Whether you read this book and apply the skills or join her communities and are guided on your own amazing journey, Lisa puts passion and purpose into everything she does. In her spare time, she's outside getting her Vitamin D working in the yard, running in her neighborhood, homeschooling her girls, or reading, often with a cup of coffee in her hands.

ACKNOWLEDGEMENTS

I am forever grateful for the people in my life and along my journey these past several years (and in some cases, my whole life).

To **Diane**, for literally carrying me, raising me, and guiding me every single day to be the strong woman I feel I've become. Oh, and raising your grandkids many times when I have a call or am writing.

To **Bill**, for giving me the ferocity to never give up, the work ethic to always push forward, and the heart to always help. Thanks for all that you do for me.

To **Matt**, for being the best part of me, giving me my two little girls that I cherish, and for always listening to my crazy and wild ideas. I've always felt we are better together.

To **Kevin**, for being the pain in my side but also someone so dramatically important by my side. I'm always proud to call you my brother.

To **Morgan**, for knowing my voice so damn well that no one can tell us apart (almost like we are sisters!). You always paint my vision and words in such a beautiful, positive light, and I'm grateful for you believing in my passion and joining in with me. Oh, and thanks for the cutest, most wonderful nephew ever!

To **Jennifer**, for always holding me accountable and believing in me. You are more important to me than you will ever know.

To **Alisa**, for pushing me to create a vision that would impact and fulfill. You have always seen the best in me and have granted me the ability to now see the best in myself.

To **Cris**, for raising the love of my life and always being excited for where we are going next in our lives.

To **Erica**, for believing in what I have to offer the world and helping me get there. If it weren't for you, no one would ever hear from me, and I appreciate you so much in friendship and beyond!

To **Michael**, for listening to me for hours go on about my financial dreams and not thinking I am crazy (or not voicing it), and always believing and supporting The Daughter Diaries' legacy.

To **Lorraine**, for always capturing my family in a beautiful light and making my visions become a reality to share with the world.

To **Melissa**, for picking up the pieces and running with it! We are making this vision possible!

THANK YOU TO MY TRIBE FOUNDERS
FOR BELIEVING IN THIS MISSION:

Amy Sue Lovas	Heather Wolff	Dorsey Palermini
Isabela Ataide	Bria Ledesma	Kim Bain
Marielle Klagmann	Amanda Reed	Jennifer Morshead
Bec Honeck	Eva Castle Goodman	
Ruthann Erdmann	Melissa Hoffman	

THANK YOU TO THE FOLLOWING SUPPORTERS OF OUR
IFUNDWOMEN CAMPAIGN AND HELPING MAKE THIS POSSIBLE!

GOLD SPONSORS:

Bethanne Packard

Marielle Klagmann, owner of It's a Bling Thing by Marielle featuring Park Lane Jewelry

Dorsey Palermini, owner of All About The Sass & Style by Dorsey

Rebeccah Johnson, owner of Blue Farms Beauty

Cris Autry

BACKERS & CONTRIBUTORS OF THE CAMPAIGN:

Melissa Hoffman	Megan Tessmer	Jennifer Morshead
Bria Ledesma	Abby Garrison	Christina Bluhm
Eva Castle Goodman	Alisa Manjarrez	Brittney Hancox

Ashley Walton	Britny Lee	Christina Hernandez
Debbie Clark	Amanda Reed	Lisa McGee
Karen Langston	Natalie Jones	Lal Owen
Erica Magarian	Kim Bain	Laura Cooper
Allie Paul	Amie Painter	Jen Albano
Chelsea Rasmussen	Heather Wolff	Michael Manjarrez
Crystal Childers	Lisa Slater	Kimberly Meese
Amy Sue Lovas	Stephanie Chapman	

Alysia Lyons *Mom Support Coach & Author of Good Moms Don't: Lies, Truths and How to Conquer Mom Guilt*
alysialyons.com | coachalysialyons@gmail.com

Megan Kirby *Marriage Coach*
megan-kirby.com

Alisa Manjarrez *Vision Producer*
thehappycactus.club

Erica Magarian *Outreach Manager*
magarian.creative.solutions@gmail.com

Michael Manjarrez *Wealth Adviser*
m.manjarrez@me.com

Tula XII Custom Life Organizer
tulaxii.com/autry

Millionaire Mamas Club
thedaughterdiary.com/services/mmc

Mamas Unstoppable Tribe
thedaughterdiary.com/services/tribe

To Gain Access to Any of My Other Services
thedaughterdiary.com/services

HOW I LIVE MY VALUES DAILY

1. **Health** - Maintain Portion Fix and work out at 4:30 p.m. daily

2. **Family** - Thirty minutes of quality time for each member of my family daily

3. **Meaningful Work** - Write for thirty minutes every single day

4. **Safety / Security** - Balance finances every night and keep tidy/cleaning schedule

5. **Education** - Read for fifteen minutes daily and homeschool (I'm learning too!)

My Intentional Transformation

_____

_____

_____

_____

_____

_____

_____

_____

_____

_____

_____

_____

_____

_____

_____

_____

Pursuing My Passion

30 DAYS OF REFLECTION OF PASSION PURSUIT

Notes for Reflection

Notes for Reflection

Notes for Reflection

Notes for Reflection

Notes for Reflection

Notes for Reflection

Notes for Reflection